Across the Street Around the Corner
...A Road Home

Also by MARY LEA CARROLL

Saint Everywhere: Travels in Search of the Lady Saints

Somehow Saints: More Travels in Search of the Saintly

Across the Street Around the Corner

...A ROAD HOME

MARY LEA CARROLL

CLYDE custom publishing

Portland, Oregon

Published by Clyde Custom Publishing
4207 SE Woodstock Blvd., Suite 253
Portland, OR 97206
www.clydecustompublishing.com

Library of Congress Cataloging-in-Publication Data is on file with the publisher.

Cover Design by Sean Paul Lavine
Page Design and Layout by Deja Nick

ISBN: 979-8-9895915-2-7

Printed in China

"While the spirit of neighborliness was important on the frontier because neighbors were so few, it is even more important now because our neighbors are so many."

- Lady Bird Johnson

Foreword

By **Thomas Schumacher**

Neighborhoods are part of us; the ones we grew up in, the fantasy ones we came to love on television as children and the ones we learn about in the pages of books. And yet in recent times, under confusing and rapidly changing conditions, we came to wonder if the world outside our doors was still what we knew.

The delightful Mary Lea Carroll opens her door and takes a walk through a neighborhood I once knew well and makes it all more heartwarming, reassuring, truthful and genuinely wonderful than I could have imagined.

Having known Mary Lea for over 40 years, including an all too brief time as her actual neighbor, I have always enjoyed seeing the world through her particular lens. Reading *Across the Street Around the Corner* filled my heart with hope and joy and confidence that just outside my door is a world I still very much want to join.

Few folks who are old enough to get a discount at the movies can say they literally live in the neighborhood that was the setting for their childhood, but this intimate relationship to the streets, houses and even some of the characters makes this reflection on our relationship to our environment all the more delicious.

The best hosts open their doors to welcome us in and make us feel right at home. Mary Lea opens her door and says, "Let's take a walk," and don't you know it, she makes you feel right at home there too.

Thomas Schumacher, producer of
The Lion King, is the chief creative
officer of Disney Theatrical Group.

Contents

To Glenn, Grace, Rose, and their friends.

Introduction

Summer 2020

As the months of the pandemic deepened in 2020, what I continually thanked my lucky stars for was our Pasadena neighborhood of quiet streets and easy sidewalks. The arching camphor trees, easily a hundred years old, stand in the parkways casting their precious shade over everything. We're an older Los Angeles-area neighborhood full of an eye-catching combination of Spanish, Tudor, Craftsman and Mid Century style homes, big ones and little ones all mixed together like a cocktail party of 20th century building styles.

It was just 35 years ago that Bill and I bought our first house here. We were newly married and couldn't know it would become our lifelong place to be. In those days, the city threatened to rezone this area for apartment blocks. We were "above the freeway," which used to mean not as good as "below the freeway" and therefore ripe for bulldozing. In truth, many a house did have bars on the windows, and neglected yards. Petty crime did emanate from a few houses and a vagabond slept in a house someone had tried to flip. But our new neighborhood felt full of rag-tag charm and that wonderful and elusive thing, potential. We joined the old-timers who organized a neighborhood association to fight this rezoning and in so doing preserved a place full of old trees and spacious yards. A perfect place to settle-in, raise a family and have a good time—which is just what Bill and I did. Our first house was a little bungalow on Catalina Street. And then, five years later, we bought a big old Dutch Colonial two blocks away that was just begging for TLC. Indeed, every single system of this lovely old money-pit needed redoing: roof, chimney, sewer, plumbing, electrical—but it offered a covered front porch, lots of space for children and a yard that eventually we filled with roses.

Now, we are the old-timers. Stepping out onto these sidewalks throughout the pandemic allowed me to ramble wherever I wanted, without actually going anywhere at all. I joined the waves of neighbors who also felt the pull just to be out in the open air. These walks were not exercise per se but small travels to be in the world. No, not the same as the travels for the writing of my two previous books, which took me to the watery alleyways of Venice for the relics of St. Bakhita or the cobblestones of Quebec in search of St. Ursula or even, the dizzying boulevards of Mexico City to see the cloak of Guadalupe. But these small rambles were the best one could do during the lockdown. Can't travel the world? Well, let's travel the neighborhood.

On these little out-and-abouts, I noticed baskets of fresh-picked citrus on people's walkways with "Help Yourself" signs. Signs in windows declaring, "Our nurses are our heroes." One neighbor set up a bookshelf and a table on his parkway and loaded it with canned goods, dish soap, cold cereal— you name it—adding to it daily. The sign read, "Free. Not the table. Not the shelf." I often saw cars pulling over to add to the collection, more than to take away. This little pop-up has now been offering free goods for more than two years. As the months wore on, some neighbors clearly went stir crazy. One house set up themed kiddy pools on their front lawn and frolicked in twelve inches of water. Adults they were, not kids. Some days their theme was tropical, sometimes straight-up party. Wearing goofy sunglasses—waving and laughing, they'd get us motorists to honk. Their plastic martini glasses cheered me on an average kinda crappy pandemic Tuesday. Thank you, crazy neighbors.

For the past months, I'd felt like I was swimming, if not drowning in time. Now retired and the kids grown and gone, and all the events to support the most recent book having been cancelled, I spent hours a day just strolling around my neighborhood, noticing what others were doing to get through the lockdown. It's almost hard to remember now how empty the days seemed; everything closed, everyone behind masks or windows or doors...everywhere.

So many of the saints I'd written about seemed to whisper to me while walking. Was I doing anything to make life a little easier for anyone besides my family? Instead of hunkering down, couldn't I strive for more thoughtfulness to those around me, the people stuck at home the way I was? Didn't others feel restless? Off-kilter?

Well, the roses in my yard were blooming away, totally unworried by the global calamity around them. Couldn't they be offered to cheer a neighbor? What about cooking big meals again and offering dinner to someone, even a random someone? (I found the easy part—cooking. The not so easy part—offering, as people seemed afraid of one another.)

And before the pandemic, when out on the sidewalk if a neighbor paused to say hi, usually I'd keep it brief—hurry on—after all, who isn't in a hurry? But now, it occurred to me that even speaking from six feet apart was an opportunity to offer someone full attention. This surprisingly tiny step was challenging. It may not have looked different to other people, but it was different for me. A tiny baby step.

I decided to challenge myself to take some kind of baby step every day toward being in the world in—I don't know, a kinder, better way. It could be a way to participate in my surroundings, appreciate where I was and be glad for good health. Let's make it a daily practice. Why not write it down, these baby steps, and keep a little diary to see if progress could be made?

Walking the sidewalks I'd known for years, ideas of neighborhood and how together we create a good, even loved, place to live grew in my mind. I wanted to talk to others to hear from them, what they've done over time to increase the value of a place—not simply the price of the real estate, but the meaningfulness of community. I started tracking down old friends and neighbors, some who I hadn't connected with for years and years. People who, in their own ways, have woven where they live into a cherished place to call home.

This renewed interest in neighborhood also sent me down the road of memory, to the neighborhood of my own childhood, which is only two miles away. The years in the big white house on Santa Rosa in Altadena with my eight brothers and sisters, my old movie-star grandmother, my exhausted parents, and the neighbor lady who changed my life forever. Roads not traveled for sixty years. All put together, these conversations, inspirations, observations, and memories became this little book.

That love thy neighbor thing? I meant that.

—God

Hello, Neighbor

Hmm, what's up for the week? Referring to my agenda, I laughed— *wow, how will I squeeze in all this nothing?* Coffee at Michelle's—cancelled. Fundraiser at the Pasadena Playhouse—off. Doctor's appointments—all x'ed. But today *was* the day to connect with Brenda. She had been my across-the-street neighbor for twenty years. We'd finally found a date and arranged to have a late-afternoon glass of wine on the front lawn, the way we used to when our kids were little, only now at a six-foot distance.

When she lived across the street, Brenda wrote copy for our annual home tours. She would show up at the meetings to hash out traffic issues. Brenda has a big PR career and her life-style sort of defines the word *busy* so I wanted her perspective on that unseen knack of creating a good neighborhood.

"This is like old times," she said with a laugh as we settled ourselves into folding chairs on the lawn. It did feel old fashioned, having the time to sit and visit with a neighbor you don't see very often. I poured us each a glass of wine.

The first time we met, we were both six months pregnant, she with her first, me with my last. Brenda and

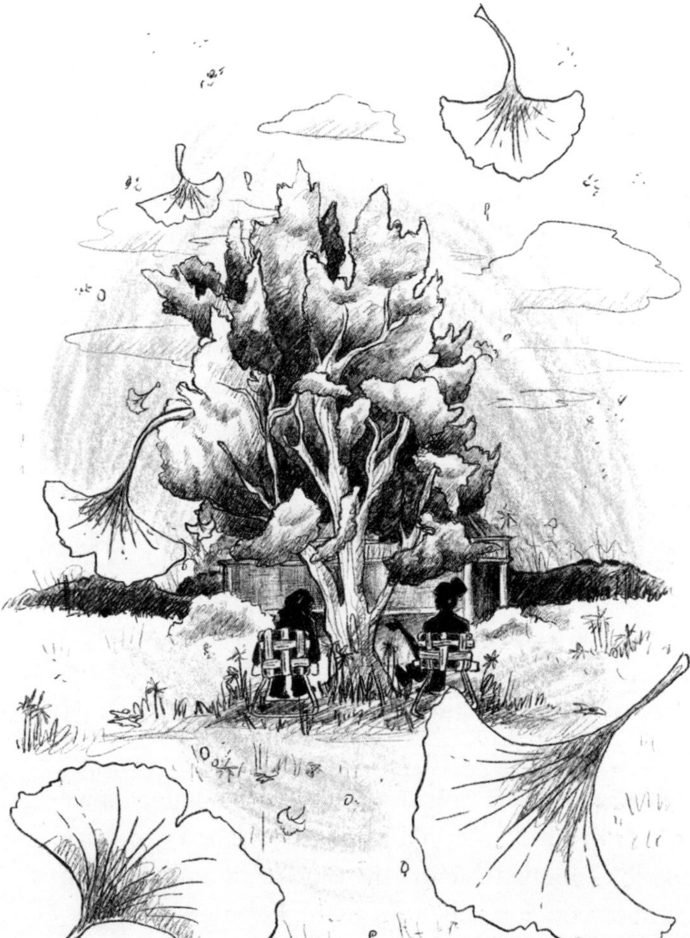

her former husband, Jim, were trying to decide whether to buy the house across the street. Was it the right place for them? Would they be happy here? Their savvy realtor had walked them around to meet who their potential new neighbors might be and so, they rang my doorbell. That's how we met. Thirty years ago.

"Oh my gosh, it's been so long," I said, settling in. "Remember the summer of the eclipse?"

"Of course! Gabe was in 8th grade."

"So was Rosie. Remember how we sat up all night—you and me on those steps," I said, pointing to our front steps.

"And all the neighbor kids in sleeping bags across the lawn," Brenda said. "All of us watching the moon disappear at midnight. . ." We both held the memory of that warm night, of how easily that slumber party sprang to life, of how our kids and those others are now grown up and of, how time passes so.

I'd asked Brenda to think about my neighborhood ponderings.

"After you called," she said, "I sat down, thought about it, and even made notes." Brenda cheerfully whipped out a piece of paper from her pocket and read, "Making where you live a place of value never just happens. You've got to be deliberate; make a conscious decision that yes, I will contribute to the spirit of this place, involve myself."

"I know," I said. "But what if a person's very shy?" She tilted her head as if to say—*yeah but you still have to.* I played devil's advocate. "Of course, if your house were on fire, anyone would run to the neighbors screaming, 'Help! Call the fire department!' But to simply call out 'Good morning! Nice to see you, neighbor!' as someone's headed to work can feel kind of lame."

Brenda answered, "But it's surprising how little it takes, and at a certain point we each have to choose—will I be the type to smile, to say hello?" Brenda is a pretty no-nonsense person. "And if somebody's moving in, you can't waste time thinking 'Oh, I'll get around to welcoming them next week.' We all know that if too much time passes, then it won't happen."

"But Brenda, think how busy people are today." We both took sips of wine, then choked on our laugh— "*So* busy," I said. "Covid's made everyone *so busy*!"

"Mary Lea, there's no way around it!" she said. "If you want a good, safe, fun place to live, it has to be you who helps make it that way. Besides, we need each other. Maybe not today, maybe not tomorrow, but when you may least expect it."

That reminded me of a time, years ago, when I had an emergency. Something had gotten into my eye—a bug or a large piece of dirt or something—when I was home alone with my toddler. What was it? It really hurt! My eye was getting worse. I called my neighbor three doors away, Leslie, and she was on my porch in one minute. Unflinchingly, she got up right close to me, opened my eye, saw a tiny piece of gravel, and got it out. Oh, I was so relieved! And another time, Scott, from the end of the block, showed up at my door with his five-year-old. Little William had jammed a washer onto his finger and now the finger was gigantically swollen. One look and I said, "Take him to the fire department right now! They'll have the tool to cut that washer off." With beads of perspiration covering his forehead, he'd been too stressed to think of that himself, so he rushed off with his little boy and got it taken care of.

"A simple hello is what breaks the ice," Brenda continued. "Hello is an overture for connection. It starts to create a thread, which eventually gets woven into a web. Ideally, your neighborhood is—I know it's a cliché—a web of support." We both nodded at the cliché, and the deep necessity, of this.

Brenda and I sat underneath our huge ginkgo tree, watching folks passing on the sidewalk taking their late-afternoon walks.

"I remember one time, Jim and I woke up in the middle of the night because of a loud and terrible fistfight happening right in our front yard," she said. "Two men. He ran out to see what was going on and realized it was the cousin of the young man next door. He was able to say, 'Guys, quit it. It's late.' And they did! So, because we knew them, we were not fearful or angry. We were simply concerned."

"Which is the way you'd want to feel, right?" I asked.

Brenda nodded. "Because if you know your neighbors, you can understand them. And if you can understand them, you can understand the immediate world surrounding you. Isn't that the basis of being comfortable? If you're sick or in an emergency and nobody knows? No one cares? But how could they care if they don't even know you?" "It's a trade-off, isn't it," I said in a joking way, "between having people know your business—*and having people know your business.*" We both laughed.

When our time was up, we gave each other a big air-hug and I watched her walk across the lawn, hop back into her car, and drive off to her new neighborhood.

Today, I picked some of my overflowing roses and arranged them in a jar and took them over to the fellows across the street. One of them, Ed, is a doctor. Doctors are working so hard. I didn't ring the bell. I just left them on the porch railing. Why didn't I ring the bell and hand them to him personally? But that requires a little more effort. But it would have been nicer. But was he busy? And what was the reason for bringing them in the first place? I couldn't actually say; so, in the end, just leaving them was easiest. Hopefully I won't always opt for easier.

"Them's Good People"

My dad used to say this whenever somebody did something that he really appreciated. The elderly gentleman four doors down from us, Mr. Hertel, would sometimes offer Dad a glass of his very best scotch, a small island of freedom from the cares of being the father to nine children. Or Mr. and Mrs. Brown, two doors down, would sometimes invite my parents to dinner at their country club. My dad was a man of few words, and an entire evening spent with neighbors would be summed up with, "Them's good people."

Tom and Jan, down the street, with their cheery dispositions—I appreciate them the way Dad would have. Tom's hair is grey now. Their kids have grown up and gone. But their painstakingly restored Craftsman home, which was a wreck when they got it, seemed busier now, with young people coming and going, than when their own kids were still there. We met up on the sidewalk one late afternoon, finally grabbing a chance to say hi. I wanted to show them the blooming progress of one man's amazing garden, five blocks away.

"What's new?" I began.

With a laugh, Jan said, "These days, we've got a regular boarding house. I don't know about you, Mary Lea, but we find it's so hard for kids to launch." I nodded in agreement. "Paul and Clare are out, and we've got all these bedrooms, so now we've got three college kids," Jan continued. "They've all kind of just come our way. A nursing school kid whose mom died. A young man with so much anxiety he's just had a hard time, but he's doing well now. And a good friend of Paul's, whose parents divorced." I thought, *Way ta' go, Tom and Jan—helping three other kids, not your own, get their footing.*

There was one summer, when my three girls were young, we had Sara stay with us because her parents had to be away. She was a little girl from down the street, and great friends with my daughters. When I first met Sara, she was two, and in the same preschool as my little Grace. Her parents, Ken and Rita, were newly back from their missionary teaching years in Ethiopia, and Sara was the precious gift they returned with. She'd been born in the orphanage of the compound they worked in, and they simply said, yes. Honored. That summer, when they asked if she could stay with us, we said yes, of course. Yes. For whatever reason, having an extra kid stay for a month or a year wasn't a stretch for me. But so often we need to have had the experience ourselves to understand the need to pass it on. I've always been grateful to the friends of my parents who gave me a room rent free for six months after college. I was scared to go home because what if I were too ill prepared to ever move on? Those 'feel good' college degrees can leave a person thinking, "Oh no, now what?" and their third-floor bedroom in an old San Francisco house helped me at just the right time in life.

The sunlight at five o'clock sifted through the camphor trees and brushed the San Gabriels with a purple hand. The San Gabriel mountains overlook Pasadena. Leaves crunched under our tennis shoes. "Tell me how you guys found this neighborhood," I asked. Tom and Jan had been so helpful in getting activities going in our neighborhood. Out on the sidewalk, they were always ready to talk to neighbors about anything: bathroom fixtures or contractors or who to call when tree roots made the sidewalks bumpy. It's this kind of presence that builds the web to get things going. Tom even stepped up to be our neighborhood association president.

"We moved here from our first little house twenty-five years ago," Tom began. "When we first got married, we lived in a tiny house on a big, busy street, sandwiched between apartments. No sense of neighborhood at all. None. I won't ever forget the day we moved here. Kellye, a woman from across the street, came over and said hello. It's funny to say that now, but we never had anybody say hello in the other house. We didn't know one single person."

"But here, a lot of people came by to say hello when they saw the moving van," Jan said, taking over. "And two weeks later, the elderly lady at the end of the block hosted a wine and cheese on her driveway just for us, so we could really meet everybody. Remember Emily?" I nodded at the memory of Emily. Strange, I'm probably the same age as Emily was then. Back then, she was the old lady on the street, and she'd made it her business to host a wine and cheese for whoever moved in.

"We felt so lucky, like we'd found the best place ever to live," Tom said. "But also it showed us that oh, this is what you do. It seems natural, a small thing, but we'd never experienced neighbors welcoming us, and I don't know if we'd do it if we hadn't ever had it happen to us."

Years ago, Kellye herself told me that the day she and David moved onto our street and were trying to get a hanging basket of geraniums up on a hook on the front porch, a neighbor came over and said, "Hi. Welcome. Want some help?" And Kellye said her first thought was, *what does she want from us?* No one had ever talked to them, let alone welcomed them, in their old neighborhood either. Emily, Kellye, Tom, and Jan. How far back can we trace these welcoming moves?

"How much cooperation do you have with each other in your block?" I asked Tom and Jan. They both chuckled. "Well, Mike has that full woodworking shop," Tom said. "He's helped with our kids' school projects forever."

"There was the time we had a weekend getaway," Jan recalled. "Clare was in high school and wasn't supposed to have friends over but. . . ya know, she did. Later, she said she'd only invited eight friends, but word got out and all these kids showed up. It got loud, kids were running through the house and yard very out of control, and Clare got scared. Well Mike and Ann, next door, called the police. They said how Clare was a good kid and so when the police got there, they broke it up in a less harsh way. And I was so glad Mike and Ann *didn't* call us. But when we got home, they very gently said, 'You know, you might want to ask Clare about the party she had.' Not 'Oh my god!' Not alarmist. Just calm. I've always been grateful for how she and Mike handled it."

Tom added, "Chris, on the corner." Chris and his wife live in a small yellow house with a towering oak in front. They work in science. "Chris took my grandmother's chest of drawers and refinished it for me. He just offered, for free. He said he wanted a project that would take a long time, something that was quiet and would help while he processed his father's passing." I thought to myself, I know what that's like. When my brother Jeff died, I fell to making jewelry, earrings specifically, day and night, night and day, for two years, until practically every friend had several pairs and local boutiques said "no more please, we're good." It had taken two years of a quiet, repetitive pursuit to process his passing. . .

❋

Before long, we arrived at the special garden. There must have been a house somewhere, but all we could see from the sidewalk were blooming roses up on a berm surrounding a circle of grass. A birdbath sat in the middle of the grass, which was also surrounded, all along its base, with seasonal gifts: eight-foot-tall sunflowers in the summer, five-foot-tall dahlias in the fall. Not to mention the columbine, the Japanese maples, the variegated canna, the thicket of papyrus, the tulips, the hyacinths. Oh, the grace, the care it all exhaled into the world. On one of the worst Southern California fire days this past summer, I saw a woman kneeling in the grass in this sidewalk sanctuary. "Are you the owner?" I asked, and she replied, "Oh no, I just come here to meditate. The owner, he said I could." Of course the man who created something like this would allow a stranger to meditate here.

Tom, Jan, and I stood there basking in the surprise and beauty of this little garden that seemingly had no house attached to it. "This guy puts a lot of work into this," Tom said. "Wonder who he is." We took a nice long look at the things in bloom before turning to retrace our route. In parting they said, "Great to see you. Thanks for reaching out. It's been way too long." I nodded in agreement, and they headed on another block to their home.

A few days later I walked by again. Oh my gosh, he was there—the elusive man who plants and tends the garden! I'd wanted to meet him for two years and there he was, poking around behind all the roses. Older, tranquil, and bespectacled, he quietly pruned away. "Hello? Oh, hello," I called out. Calmly he looked up. "Are you the owner?" He smiled and nodded. "I've wanted to meet you for so long, what's your name?"

"Robbie," he said with ease.

"Good to meet you, Robbie. Your garden is wonderful. I just love it," I gushed.

"Appreciate it," he said with a smile. "I'm a little late on everything this year." He completely paused to talk to me, not in any hurry at all.

"I only noticed your garden about two years ago. Have you been doing it long?"

"Oh, since about the mid-'90s," he said with a smile.

I blinked, realizing how long ago that was. Wanting to keep the conversation going, I added, "You have so much amendment built up all around. Do you constantly keep adding more, or was it a huge one-shot thing?"

"Actually, there's asphalt under this," he said. "Back in the '90s, the city scraped the street and just dumped the rubble here. The people I bought it from parked cars on top of the rubble." I took in the glistening grass, the hyacinths breaking through the black soil, the meticulously placed sticks that will support the forthcoming spring display. "So when I got it, I just covered everything over with soil. Dig deep enough and you'll get to the broken concrete and asphalt."

Look what he did: took rubble and gave us Eden. Now, them's good people.

My oldest daughter, Glennie, gave me the idea when she said people were doing this up where she lives, in San Francisco. So, I too started putting a basket of refreshments on the front porch—chips, sodas, fresh fruit, protein bars—for the delivery people who come to my door: UPS, DoorDash, FedEx, you name it. The pandemic's making them work nonstop. The basket looks so welcoming with its little "Help Yourself" sign. Why didn't I think of this myself instead of having to be told about it? Either way, putting it together and putting it out there made me feel unexpectedly proud, like I was living the way I want to be living.

The Kids on the Corner

My old friend and neighbor Ben Yandell used to say a happy childhood was an inoculation against life's hardships. To that, I'd add that a happy neighborhood makes that inoculation even more effective.

With four children already, my parents bought the big Georgian colonial on the corner of Mendocino and Santa Rosa in 1952 and then proceeded to have five more of us. When my grandfather died, Dad converted the garage into a cozy house for Ruthie, Mom's mother, so she'd be just a garden walk away. Ruthie worked until she was eighty-two selling newspaper ads. But she'd once been a bona-fide silent movie star, from 1914 to 1919, and even though it was 1960, in her mind, it could've been yesterday. To Ruthie's dying day, her nails were done and her bubble hairdo just so. She tried to never miss an afternoon at the racetrack. The friends of ours who spent their childhoods in and out of our house still tell stories about her. Everyone laughed at her driving—well, she didn't learn until she was fifty-nine—and her hearing was terrible. Also, she had very little filter. Every time Mom got pregnant, Ruthie would cry out, "You're ruining your life with all these kids!" But Mom knew when not to listen—like every evening, while she toiled away making dinner for twelve, and Ruthie sat after she got home from the track, watching her daughter work, sipping her gimlet, and offering unsolicited opinions on how rude drivers were, how gawdawful hippies looked, on the sky high price of a good steak...

Santa Rosa Avenue was just a mile long, with eighty-foot deodar trees marching up and down both sides. Deodars are giant Christmas trees with some limbs reaching out like the necks and backs of horses. As children, we'd climb and sit on the horses' backs, watching the cars pass beneath, and by kicking the tree limb, we could get the horses to fly. . . To this day, the smell of cedar wood and the feel of that sticky bark still sends me up, up, and away. And magically— from Thanksgiving to New Year's—volunteers would string each tree with hundreds of lights and our street became known far and wide as Christmas Tree Lane, a mile-long tunnel of lights. It continues to this day, with the trees even taller now. How we loved standing at the end of our driveway, trying to out shout each other as the cars streamed by to admire the lights. "Merry Christmas!! Ho-ho-ho! Hap-Hap-Happy New Year!" we'd shout until our throats were so sore that the only medicine was more peppermint candy canes.

We did not have sidewalks, but we did have big river-rock gutters that were three feet deep. All the driveways up and down the street had little cement bridges spanning these gutters, which created tunnels underneath. In summer we'd scrabble around in them, daring one another. Jeff, who was three years older than me, would say,

"Something's died in there, Mary Lea. Dare ya to go see." Of course, I would hesitate. "Want to read my comics? Ya gotta crawl in there." The tunnels were dark, damp, and full of spiders. Danny, who was two years older than me, would toss in, "Are you chicken? I think you're chicken." Then to show off, he'd recklessly crawl in there, calling the rest of us a bunch of babies. And it was always exciting when Ruthie ran her Corvair off the edge into a gutter, causing her to scream for help. Dad and all the boys, often including a few neighbor boys, would run out, yelling, "Ruthie's done it again!" and working together, they'd get her and the car out of the stone ditch.

We had everything we could want in our neighborhood: an ice cream and candy counter two blocks away at Thrifty's, a pet store where I bought hamster supplies, access to a swimming pool, and streets full of kids our age. A few friends stand out after all these years: Maya and Eric, the twins down the block; Carl, up the long driveway of the flag lot; the Van Der Kar kids, who raised pigeons; and Tommy Miller, my brother Danny's great friend, whose mom gave us carrot sticks on crushed ice. Walter, he was my brother Jeff's great friend—they loved putting on plays. Each of us had our best friends, and mine, when I was eight, nine, and ten, were Susan and Barbara.

The thing that stood out about being at their houses was that their mothers were so calm. Barbara's mother actually *made* the clothes for her Barbie. Susan's mother's kitchen was so clean, they even had filtered water in a big glass dispenser. Every cookie I ate at her house came

from a brand-new, unopened package. The good kind, marshmallow on graham cracker dipped in chocolate. At our house, Mom would point at a bowl of apples and shout, "Take one and *go outside*!"

Next to Susan lived the Hertels. Barbara, Susan, and I loved them. We would knock on the door and say, "Mrs. Hertel, can Herb come out and play?" She would go get her husband and he'd smile, bend down, and say, "Girls, would you like to help me trim the birds of paradise?" We'd stand there and talk to him as he got down on his knees and pruned those exotic bird-like, beast-like plants. He'd tell us about his days running a railroad. Once I overheard my father say to Mom, "You know that son-of-a-gun Herb has over $200,000 in the bank. Jeez!"

On hot summer days, if Mom went someplace, we'd take the opportunity to call the other kids to hurry over. This was our chance to play Water-Fight. It went like this: Our friends would drag garden hoses from their own yards to ours, and we'd hook them up to our numerous outdoor faucets. Then we'd break into teams and station ourselves in various parts of the yard. On the count of three, we'd blast the hoses full force, chasing and attacking each other. Screaming and yelling—who could inflict the most sopping, soaking, dead-on assault on the others? To win? The goal was to be the last ones standing after everyone else was drowned out. So much running and laughing across the lawn, running across the patio, running up the back of the house, coming round the driveway. Our feet got so tough from going without shoes that we could run barefoot down the middle of the street even after it'd been re-graveled. But oh, the instant Mom's rumbly eggplant-purple Cadillac came around the corner, everybody'd cut off the water, grab their hoses, and nonchalantly slink off for home. Our yard seemed to be the place for this kind of thing, even though everyone else had perfectly good yards.

An even more memorable game was to call the gang over for a round of Inside-Outside! With Water-Fight, Mom kind of turned a blind eye, but this game was a total big NO! Step one was to definitely get rid of Mom. A common pretext might be, "Mom, I need more glue for my school project." Of course, this wouldn't take her very long, but she always found other things to do when she was out. So, once she was safely away, kids just showed up and we'd break into two teams.

I think Jeff was the genius who thought this game up. The idea was for the inside team to go inside and do whatever they could to lock and barricade the whole house to keep the outside team from breaking in and capturing everybody. The inside team had ten seconds to run throughout, upstairs and downstairs, locking doors and windows and throwing together roadblocks—but it was a big old house, with five bedrooms, a balcony, a basement, a screen porch, and an attic, not to mention a kitchen door, a back door, and the French doors. I might be in Bethie's room with my body thrown against her door to the balcony to keep Susan out and hear Kevin hollering "Help!" as he tried to keep Danny from crawling through the girls' bathroom window. Danny would've shimmied up the pole of the carport and jumped to the balcony railing. Meanwhile, everyone else was crashing around, running up the front stairs, hurling themselves down the back stairs. If you got tagged by an outsider, that's it. You were out. Once a few outsiders had broken in, it exploded into a full-blown game of tag. The unhampered glee of this sort of play, playing with everything you've got, has stayed with me all my life.

Days or weeks later, whenever Dad discovered it, nobody would have any idea how the window got cracked, or why the doorknob screws kept falling out, or how come the bentwood kitchen chair was splintered. . . .

By the time Mom and Dad sold the house, in 1975, Jim, Sal, and Jeff were grown and out. But the rest of us—Dan, me, Kevin, John, and Beth (not Mark because he was still only fourteen)—were just livin' on easy street at home. We young-adult kids treated meals like group dinners in a commune. We came and went as we wished. Jeff and John's hair streamed below their shoulders; my parents couldn't understand torn bell bottoms, no shoes, no bra, no bigger goals than exploring peace 'n love. All this exhausted them. They'd dealt with Jeff's pot business, the boys' various car crashes, Sally's bad boyfriends. They were just worn out from the 1970s' f-you attitude.

So finally, as we enjoyed dinner one night around the kitchen table, expounding on how awful Richard Nixon was, Dad abruptly put down his napkin and said, "Okay, look, you characters, time's up. Your mother and I have decided to sell the house, so you"—here he fluttered his hands— "you all go do something. Shoo. Shoo now." We were shocked that they could do such a thing! But we did, in pretty quick order, find our next steps in life. Within six months, the house was sold, and my parents waved "bye-bye now" and moved away. (My dad took a job in another city.) We laugh about it now, how it was Mom and Dad who left home because they simply couldn't get rid of us. My poor parents, oh my gosh, God bless them.

When I was in my thirties and forties, with children of my own, the memory of those carefree years made it difficult for me to ever say *No, don't, stop!* when Glennie, Grace, or Rose wanted to "fire up the mud hole," thereby flooding the walkway. When five or six of their little friends raced back and forth across the front lawn, crushing a plant or shrub, I never had the heart to tell them to knock it off. *Play* is what I'd say in my heart. *Play as long and as hard as you can.*

May I Borrow an—Oops!

There isn't a lot of risk in borrowing a cup of sugar. What could go wrong? Break the cup the sugar was in? And borrowing and lending is part of creating the web of support that a neighborhood can provide. Here are a few gleanings from my walks and talks with neighbors.

❋

"It's funny now, but I ruined all my neighbor's battery-operated candles that she lent me. I kept trying to light them with a match."

❋

"I'd never seen a digital thermometer before. In an emergency, I borrowed a thermometer from my neighbor for the Thanksgiving turkey. I didn't know the red plastic sheath came off and so I rammed the entire thing into my bird. OMG, when I took the turkey out of the oven, the red sheath was gone. . . it had melted away."

❋

"We lent our neighbors a little inflatable boat. It got popped on the Merced River in Yosemite. They felt so bad they insisted on buying us a new one. I said, *No, don't, please, we never use it anymore.* But they did buy us a new one. The new one sat in the garage, and we finally put it out with all the other stuff when we had a yard sale. Guess who bought it? Yes, the family who'd given it to us a few years earlier. We had to haggle over the price when they were going to pay the twenty bucks I had it listed for. Finally, I won. They paid $1."

With everyone spending so much time at home, it seems like all the closets, kitchens, and garages are getting cleaned out. While on my walk this morning, I came upon a bunch of great stuff piled on the parkway. I knew for a fact that my neighbor, Jean, was wanting a wooden cutting board. She'd become afraid that her plastic ones were shedding micro-plastics—and here was a big one of beautiful oak, right here, leaning against a tree. But so heavy! I'd have to carry it five blocks. But I was filled with delight at the thought of her coming home and just finding it on her porch. But it was so heavy. It'd be gone if I waited until I went for the car. . . But it's so heavy. But—okay. I picked it up and lugged it home, enduring the curious looks from motorists. . . just why is *that small woman hauling a huge cutting board down the street? Still makes me laugh.*

A Gatekeeper

Our middle daughter, Gracie, pretty much left home for good the day she went to college. But when she was little, she seemed to own Topeka Street, along with her best friend Sara. They had their select camphor trees for climbing up into. They had their dog walking business. Gracie was a competitive Girl Scout cookie seller. She rescued kittens. Together with her other close-in friends, she'd go on adventures to the drive-through dairy to buy popsicles and candy. Our girls all went to St. Elizabeth's, only two blocks away, and so they walked. When Bill and I bought our bigger house, just two blocks from our first little house, it was important to me that it be close to where they'd go to school. For me, walking to school *is* school.

When I was a child, this is how I walked the three blocks by myself, to kindergarten: Head out the screen porch door, cross the lawn, duck through the bushes to Ruthie's driveway, and cross Santa Rosa. Take the one block of Berry Place, then turn down toward the man with the pigeon coop. Pass his thorny bushes and head up the steps to Altadena Elementary and into Miss Patty's kindergarten class. In first grade, I got to wear a uniform and join my sibs on the mile-and-a-half walk to St. Elizabeth's. A child never thinks she is too young for independence.

When talking to Gracie on the phone the other day, she reminded me of how quirky apartment living can be. "I answered an ad to find my first apartment after college," she started. "A Chinese girl named Daisy accepted me as a housemate." It interested Grace to learn that her whole family had converted to Mormonism when they emigrated to the U.S., simply because an immigration pamphlet called *Making a New Life in America* said a good way to get comfortable in your new land was to join a church. A church was at the end of the block of the first place they landed. Daisy's family went down to see what church was like in America. Everyone there was so friendly, inviting them to barbecues and house parties and they thought *wow*, Mormonism is great! America is great! Could the difference between loving a place and hating a place be that simple?

Grace's first apartment had about ten units and was pretty neglected. A big corporation owned it and they didn't care. Berkeley is strange that way—the rents are sky high, and the land is so valuable, but the buildings can be rundown. She went on to recount, "We got in and out of the building through a black metal security gate, and an old man stood there all day long. His clothes were worn out, and he seemed sketchy, but he'd say hi and open and close the gate for you."

Turns out, she learned, he'd lived there a long time. He was retired now so this gate was kind of his little world. He kept an eye on who came and went, kept an eye on the neighborhood, kept an eye out against crime. "He'd say, *'How ya doing?'* and give a smile and let you in," she said.

Often other old people passed by and paused to talk with him. Sometimes there'd be a whole group of old people standing around the gate, socializing. "I ended up relying on him. The simple fact that he was always there and would smile made me feel good. It made this rundown apartment a nicer place to live," Grace said.

I once read a list of ways to create a warmer atmosphere in any neighborhood. It can be as simple as turning on your porch light at night. Or spending time in the front yard. Picking up trash when it's right in front of you. If you find yourself thinking, *someone ought to do something about that*—could that person be you?

Sat out front on the lawn and kept an eye on the city crew as they cut down the enormous camphor tree in the parkway. Years of drought had been too much for it. The city had sent out an hydraulic lift, a truck for grinding limbs into sawdust and four guys with chainsaws. My 100-year-old camphor wasn't going to go easily. The night before, I went out and with all my might hugged my tree goodbye, pressing myself into its trunk and thanking it for being outside my window and for hiding the telephone pole and for giving so much shade.

Now, with the chainsaws in full swing, healing odors of camphor oil stung my nostrils and I thought about the fact that camphor trees survived the atomic blast in Hiroshima. (Not the above-ground part, but the root systems sent up shoots very quickly.) In Hiroshima, they're called "survivor" trees, and in Japan, once a camphor reaches 100 years of age it's believed to become inhabited by healing, protective Totoros, *or spirits, and from then on are called Spirit Trees.*

The heaviest limbs of my tree crashed down and crushed the sidewalk as they hit. Boom. 100 years. And boom. 100 years. And boom. I was the only one out witnessing this event. I am glad to be of an age old enough to know; plant another one quickly and it won't take too long to grow. I'd have never been so accepting when younger.

When the crew left, a mother from down the block and her two little ones came by and studied the mountain of sawdust and the flat stump that was wide as a hot tub. They were just looking. Didn't they want to play? I got out of my lawn chair and went over and climbed up onto the stump myself. "Isn't it great? It's big enough to dance on!" I said to little Olivia and Florian. "Come up with me! Want a bag to take some of this sawdust home?" They did not want to dance with the exuberant neighbor lady, but they did want to climb up and stand there with me, and they did want the sawdust. In the following days, I saw them often scrabbling around the enormous trunk.

Etched Memories

My brothers Jim, Jeff, Dan, Kevin, John, and Mark all had paper routes. On Sundays, a man would drive by about 4:30 in the morning and dump bundles of the *Star-News* at the end of our driveway. The boys would start at 5 a.m.— sitting in the dark cold, tri-folding each one and sliding a rubber band around it. They'd pack their canvas bags, which hung from both sides of their handlebars, and take off by 5:45. Thirty papers each, and each would head in a different direction. Much of it was straight uphill. That's how Altadena is, straight uphill until the roads dead-end into the mountains. They'd make several trips back to reload their bags. I believe they all actually hated delivering papers, but how else to make money?

During a lull in the pandemic, my brothers Dan and Kevin and I had breakfast together in Altadena; a rare thing since Dan lives in Phoenix and Kevin in Paso Robles. Me, I never left our town. "Let's take a drive for old time's sake," I proposed after we'd had bacon and eggs at Fox's—the little diner popular in 1960 and still popular as I write now in 2022. The place my brother Jeff had his first job and got fired from when he let a bunch of pies burn. The place my mother and her girlfriends had Friday lunch once a month.

They'd order their fish sandwiches and then do their Fox's ritual: Slap their hand on the table and say, "Go." One of them would start, pouring her heart out about a problem, usually either with a child or her marriage. All of these women had at least five children, so there was a lot to seek advice on. This was before shrinks, when women relied only on each other to get through troubles. Fox's, good old Fox's, still with red vinyl chairs.

After paying our bill, we hopped into my Subaru and headed up Lake Avenue past Altadena Hardware, owned back then by old man Macintyre, who fell in love with Ruthie. We kids couldn't believe that such a bald, old man would come to our front door with flowers and that our grandmother would go out to dinner with him.

"Let's follow my paper route," Danny said. Okay! We headed further up toward the San Gabriel Mountains, past the house Mom grew up in on Pine Street, and where, on the same block, she saved her best friend Winnie's life, when she and Winnie were fourteen. "Remember," Kevin said, "Mom told the story over and over—one Friday night, Winnie had to babysit, and Mom had nothing to do, so she went around to check to see if Winnie'd gotten the kids to bed yet. Maybe they could play cards. Mom rang and rang the bell and finally went around to look through the windows. Winnie was asleep on the couch. So early? Bang, bang on the window. Nothing. So, Mom had the wherewithal to crawl through the window. What she found was that Winnie and the little kids weren't asleep—no!

They were unconscious from a gas leak! And Mom saved them all."

"I never heard that story..." Danny said.

"That's because you never had to ride around with Mom when she delivered Christmas cards," Kevin said.

We passed the house where our great Aunt Ruby and great Aunt May had been the block captains during World War II. It still looks the same: a wood frame house with steps up to the front porch and bushes all around. Unchanged since 1944. Then down Marengo, over to Mariposa, and along a couple of side streets. At so many intersections, Danny would point, as if he were aiming a BB gun and tell us, "I was hit by a car there." And a few blocks on, "And I was hit by a car there." Kevin joined in, "And that's where Mark got hit, over there. Remember? Mrs. Denny was backing out of her driveway." We started laughing—even though it was horrible. "Paper routes," Kevin and Dan said together.

Now we slowed down in front of our family's old place on Santa Rosa. "It's a wreck," Danny said. "That fence! Who're they trying to keep out?"

"The people who bought it had a fire," I said. "The roof is all wrong. It's never looked good since."

"There's still some roses in the front circle," Kevin said. "They've got to be 100 years old."

We craned our necks to see into the yard. "Those kick-the-can games," Danny said. "Look. The loquat trees are still back there, by Ruthie's old house." Indeed they were, the small trees we'd used as a free post in that ruckus game. We kept driving, over to Calaveras, passing Mrs. McKay's place, or actually the blah houses her five acres had been subdivided into decades ago. "The sheep and ponies," I said. "The orchard," Kevin said. "The peacocks," Dan said.

"Someday, I'm going to write a whole book about Mrs. McKay," I said. "You better," Danny said. "People won't believe it." And we drove on. . .

Finding Home

We have neighbors who moved here from Colombia seven years ago. Luisa and her husband and two little girls live at the end of the block. Not long ago, I picked her up and we went to church together, and in her elegant, accented English she told me how they found our neighborhood and their house.

"It never crossed my mind that I'd ever live in the States, ever. Even though I studied English in LA for nine months. On Fridays, to treat myself, I'd go to Old Town Pasadena. I loved to window shop there and it was a good place to meet my fellow students. That was back in 2000. And so years passed. I met my husband who was Colombian also but had grown up in LA, down in the South Bay. When he was offered a transfer to Los Angeles, I said okay— but wherever we go, it has to be near Old Town Pasadena! Our first trip here was for just five days, and we had to buy a house in that time. It was very hard. I didn't know anyone. I didn't know the culture well enough to be able to understand the neighborhoods I saw and put them into context. I knew I did not want a fixer. I did not want a pool. But I did want a neighborhood where we could feel at home.

FRAGILE
UP

"When we turned off the busy street onto Topeka, I saw right away the trees, which are so calming. The houses looked well cared for but not elaborate or too big. That made me think, 'Oh, people here are down to earth.' Because coming from Colombia, sometimes if there are statues and gates and things are very formal, you feel the people are not friendly.

"Since I really didn't know how things would work out, I began praying to the Virgin to please put me in a neighborhood where I will feel safe, where I will feel I could belong. Send me a sign. I decided if there were roses in the front, that will be my sign.

"This house we got—it *was* a fixer and it had a pool, things on my do-not-want list. But the owner was there when we went to look. He personally gave us the tour, and standing in the kitchen, he so nostalgically talked about raising his kids on this street, in the house. It moved me a great deal. And I looked out the window to see one rose bush, and it had one bloom on it."

❋

Debbie, a friend in another neighborhood, also from a big family of ten kids, looks at her golden retriever and says, "Maisie takes herself down to Indy's house and walks right in." Indy is the poodle mix two doors down. Indy's owner, Peggy, lets Indy run up to Debbie's anytime and jump in the pool. Sara Smiles, a lab-mix across the street, is at Debbie's house whenever her owners, Scott and Christy, have work meetings. "In fact," Debbie says, "all the dogs are at my house when my neighbors have work meetings or have to run to the dentist or something. They ask their dogs, *Want to go to Auntie Debbie's? Want to go to Auntie Debbie's?* And they get all excited. Thank goodness I have the kind of yard a dog cannot destroy. Sometimes there are six dogs in the pool. I get so much joy from seeing them play. The pool is not hard to clean, really..."

❋

Cynthia, a friend in yet another neighborhood further away recounted, "Our neighbor, Rob, has gotten so old and has let his yard go. I worry about Rob. We all do on this street. He used to ride his bicycle all over, but now, he shuffles down the sidewalk with a walker. I stopped by to talk to him when he was sitting out front in a plastic chair. 'Rob, would you like some help pruning back the lantana?' I asked. It was taking over the driveway and his whole porch. He said, 'Oh, no thank you. I'm letting it grow for the butterflies.' When he told me this, his yard suddenly didn't seem to need any help. It made me think, *What if everybody cared more about butterflies and less about other things?"*

❋

When I looked out and saw our neighbors got a new refrigerator and stove, and that the big cardboard boxes were strewn across their lawn, waiting to be broken down, I had an idea. I remembered how much fun my own children once had with huge boxes; they became castles and tunnels. So, I went over and dragged them to the little neighbor boys' lawn. What will they do with them? Maybe forts and spaceships? It made me happy to do this almost silly act. From our front porch, Bill called out, "Mary Lea, what the heck are you doing?" I know, I know, I thought. It reminded me to text their mom, Katie, to say it's me and not someone dumping junk. Oh my gosh, I feel for all the parents of small children who are locked down at home, no playmates, no school. . . It would've been loony-bin time for me, definitely. Maybe this will give those little boys a few hours of diversion.

Making a Place Your Place

What Tom and Jan had said about how hard it can be for kids to launch led me to think about what a challenge it is for young people wanting to buy their first house.

"You should talk to Tessa," my neighbor Pat said as we stood chatting. "She just bought a house!" Pat is proud of his daughter's career choice and her skill with money. He and his wife, Maria, have lived on the corner for 25 years. They saw the potential of this neighborhood and were not afraid to buy their house even though it had actually been given up on by the previous owners; the bathrooms and kitchen torn out, a wandering, mentally-ill man sleeping on the porch— and feral cats.

When Tessa graduated from college, she became a Teach for America teacher, a government organization sort of like the Peace Corps. She found her calling as a high school science teacher in Los Angeles. Right away she was determined to figure out a way to buy a house because she saw how houses kept going up, up, up in price. She analyzed how much it costs to own a car. She thought about how much her friends spent on eating out. Thrifty by nature and realistic about what she could afford, she found her first house within walking distance of her school and equally wisely, found a roommate to help with the mortgage.

I called Tessa up for a FaceTime visit. "For me," she began, "I grew up feeling it was normal having friends in the neighborhood and going to different houses." She talked with a huge smile. "So, in getting to know this neighborhood, I'd wave to whoever I saw hanging out on their porch or working in their garden as I walked home from work. Pretty soon, lots of people were waving to me as I passed by. I liked it. It made me feel I'd be missed, in a small way, if I were gone."

In Tessa's new neighborhood, Vietnamese and Spanish are spoken alongside English. "I have an advantage being a high school teacher," she said. "I'm not afraid of teenagers. If I see a group of kids, maybe they're smoking pot or just messing around, chances are I know them. In seven years of teaching, I can honestly say I've never met a bad kid. Ever. 100%. I have one student in jail right now and I'd still say he's a good kid," she said emphatically.

"It's a bonus that I speak Spanish," she continued, "because I am definitely the different one in my neighborhood. I didn't go around knocking on doors saying hi, hi, hi to everyone. Just waving on my way home was enough. But when Andrew and I married and he moved in, we wanted to take the neighborhood more seriously, make sure people knew who we were, so our big idea was to have a yard sale. I'm not gonna lie, it was pretty bad—we stood out there at the end of our driveway for two days, trying to sell a lot of stuff our neighbors couldn't use, and we probably made fifty bucks. But people came by to see who we were and talk. It worked. We made several neighborhood connections. I met Jorge, next door. And when I first talked with Mrs. Sanchez, across the street, I told her about how Jorge's daughter works at Disneyland. She said, 'Who? Who's Jorge?' But she now knows us, and Jorge knows us, and she knows Jorge.

"We tried again at Halloween. You know, Mrs. Carroll, what a huge deal Halloween was when we were growing up, right? So we opened our garage and got a fog machine and played scary music. We put candy into little bags and decorated them and we stood out on the driveway again, calling out 'trick or treat' to cars that slowed down to see the fog. Okay, it was a little bit lame, but hey, we did give out all the candy!

"The best neighborhood help is the little market at the end of the street," she continued. "Everybody checks in there and talks for a little bit. It creates a sense of community, which is great because just knowing there are always people nearby to chat with makes things seem nice, like I belong. . ."

The other day, I heard of a young man facing dire cancer treatments and said "Yes!" to making meals for him. I only made dinner three times for him before he had to go back in for a bone marrow transplant. It was just my pretty boring cooking—meat loaf, baked potato, broccoli, salad—but the basket of warm food felt like precious cargo as I drove it to his house. I prayed for his health as I went; it was so painful to learn that this young man had been a middle school classmate of my youngest. If anything of this sort befalls my own children, how I hope someone will drive a warm meal to them, how I hope some out of the blue parent from their childhood will pray for them.

Swimming Pools and Barbies

When I was about eight or nine, a family with a swimming pool across Santa Rosa and down another block came to light. The Boyers had a kidney-shaped pool *and* a daughter a bit older than me, Janine. She was friends with Janet, a girl on her block. Janet was friends with Barbara, who lived right behind her and they'd climb over the wall to play with one another. Now, I was friends with Barbara because her house was right next to the postbox, which was on my street. I'd often walk to the postbox for my mom, and Barbara and I became friends because she liked to play with her hamsters on the front lawn. Her brother had a hamster business. His room was *really* full of hamsters in cages. Every time one of his hamsters had babies, he'd sell them.

So, because I knew Barbara and Barbara knew Janet and Janet and Janine were friends, I got invited to swim at Janine's house. The first time Janet and Barbara took me over swimming, Janet had to warn me, "You won't believe it. Her parents don't smoke." Janet, relishing her knowledge, added, "It might be their religion. You'll see, there aren't any ash trays in the house." Barbara added quickly, "Shh. Act like it's normal."

Not smoke? At my house a Saturday morning job was to go around with a supermarket sack and empty all the ashtrays—upstairs in my parent's bedroom, the cars, the den, the kitchen. Why on earth wouldn't parents smoke? Within a few years, the surgeon general's campaign would stub this habit out across the nation, but just, not yet. In fact, when it started to be known to quit smoking, I said to Ruthie over our bowls of cereal one morning—she was studying the racing form and I was reading the want-ads for free pets—I said, "Ruthie, when are you going to quit smoking?" She looked up, cigarette poised elegantly between her fingers, "Quit? Don't be ridiculous. Anything smoking's done to me happened so long ago I've forgotten about it by now," and she took a puff.

Just before Janet rang the doorbell she whispered, "Also, Janine's parents don't drink coffee in the morning." It took a minute to wrap my small mind around such behavior from adults. But then, Mrs. Boyer opened the door and let us through to the pool. It was teeming with neighborhood kids. As an eight-year-old, to have discovered this pool so close to home seemed like winning the lottery. I jumped right in. From then on, hours and hours at a time were spent in that small pool.

To my knowledge, none of us had friends who didn't live within walking or biking distance. School friends were school friends and then, there were your regular friends—the ones whose moms made you sandwiches, the ones whose trees you could climb, the ones you rode bikes with. Eric and Maya, the twins, also had a pool but it didn't work.

Their house was one of the remaining old houses with grand columns, and their pool had, honest to goodness, come off an ocean liner. It was ten feet deep and solid iron. Its ladders were from that ship. It'd been sunk into the ground in their yard around 1920, but because it was so old, it never drained and had become a frightful, stinky swamp. We pretended it was the acid pit from the scariest movie anybody'd ever seen, *The House on Haunted Hill.* But they did have a tall, wide and spreading oak tree. A rope swing had been hung way, way up so you had to climb into the lower branches to get ahold of it. With one push you could sail so far up and away into the air. Sometimes six kids were up in that tree at once. We spent hours in their tree.

After becoming friends with Janine, then it was okay for me to invite Susan to come swimming too. Neighborhood connections sometimes took time to work out.

Susan's house was only three doors from Barbara's. Even though Susan lived so close to Barbara's brother's hamster business, she wasn't allowed to have one. Susan's house had a shag carpet in her step-down living room, which we were asked not to go into; her mother liked seeing the patterns the vacuum made in the carpet. Her mother called the couch a *davenport,* and we were asked not to sit on it. Susan's mother had blond hair and liked wearing powder blue sweaters.

Even though there were a lot of rules, I loved being at Susan's wonderland of a house, because everything there— so different from me— every appliance worked! Our broken dishwasher was used as a safe—Mom padlocked it— to lock up cookies and potato chips or maybe some birthday presents. At Susan's, theirs washed dishes. They had one really good TV, not two bad ones. At our house, the TV that only had sound, but no picture, sat on top of the second TV, which only had picture, but no sound. Then someone had to stand next to the TVs and keep touching one of them so we could get reception. At Susan's, we simply headed into her TV den, where her brother watched *American Bandstand* every afternoon after school. Every teenager in America watched this show. That's how we learned dances like The Twist and The Swim, so we could be ready for that magical day in the future when we'd go to junior high. After dancing in front of the TV for a while, we'd head upstairs to play Barbies. I didn't have a Barbie, they were quite expensive then. Even girls who had everything, like Susan, would only have one Barbie. But she had every Barbie outfit under the sun, and we spent hours putting together Barbie's dreamy outfits. Everyone I knew did this. Playing Barbie, climbing trees, and swimming at Janine's. What more could there possibly be?

So, Do Good Fences Make Good Neighbors?

The other day I met up with Ursula, from a little North of us. She has recently retired from a career in law—and doesn't seem one bit sad about it. "We're very lucky," Ursula said as we began our walk. "There are only nine houses on our cul-de-sac. I believe that has something to do with how close-knit we are. I have no idea how the name 'Throbbing Rose' came about, but that's what we've called it for years. Friday afternoon a text goes out— 'Hey, who's around tonight? Let's get together.' Prior to Covid, we spent so many Friday evenings meeting up with each other. We still get together regularly for social occasions, but our lives and work patterns changed with the pandemic. Our emergency safety meetings still happen, to make sure we all know how to take care of not just our own, but our neighbor's property, as well." Hearing her describe her block made me happy to realize how well they seemed to work together.

"We and our next-door neighbors, Tracy and Robin, keep our back doors open," Ursula continued. I smiled. . . open doors, not locked up tight. . . take a breath. In Ursula's end of the neighborhood, no camphor trees stand watch over the street. No, it's more palms and a variety of whatever owners planted, sycamores, jacaranda, avocado, plenty of citrus. We headed out for a walk. The brisk and early air brought out so many birds, and they sang to us and to each other as we strolled . . .So much beauty abounds right at the start of a new day. "And we go in and out of each other's houses and get whatever we might need. Corkscrew? Tylenol? A certain sized cooking pot? My daughter babysat for Tracy and Robin's children, and before their children graduated college, they house-sat and dog-sat for my daughter!" It's startling to realize how swiftly time passes, especially with children; the growing, the going, and the coming back.

Everyone on the cul-de-sac has an open invitation to enter Paul and Stanislava's backyard and use the pool when they want. No need to call ahead." Our walk took us swiftly one block after the next this tranquil Tuesday morning. "When my marriage broke up everybody on the street looked after me, made sure I had meals, made sure I had as much company as I needed. And one summer, when Tracy's daughter came home from college and needed a car for work, she and her family used my extra."

"You gave your car to your neighbor's daughter for the summer?" I asked, as if I hadn't heard her correctly. Ursula nodded. "But weren't you afraid something would happen?"

"It's a *car!*" she said. "I'm insured."

What a way to live. To know we have enough of everything; that life is safe enough to be easy-going with our car, our house keys, our swimming pool. How affirming to have this ease. How comforting to know those around you would go out of their way to make sure you are doing well.

❋

Leslie was my neighbor three doors down, but then moved three blocks away to a larger home for their growing kids. Several neighbors in our area have done that— when they could afford it, moved to a bigger house only a block or two away. Leslie recounted something she has never forgotten. "We were coming home from a camping vacation. The kids were little, the drive had been long. We were tired and it was late and all the unpacking had to be done. But our neighbor, Olga, who'd watched the house while we were away, just showed up as we were unloading the car and had a full dinner for us—a roasted chicken, salad, vegetables and even dessert. Everything! We were so deeply amazed by her thoughtfulness. She just said, 'Oh it's nothing, really,' as she handed us this yummy food. Her 'oh it's nothing' is a kindness that has stayed with me all these years. What a memorable thing for my neighbor to do."

Leslie and her husband, Mitch, made a big change a few years ago to their front yard: "We put in eight olive trees where the front lawn used to be. It took a few years for them to grow, but now we have a friends-and-neighbors olive picking party. It's a full day, with food, music, and drinks. We want everyone to have fun while working on the harvest. Everybody helps in some way. We live in a city and hardly anyone has the opportunity to feel nature in this basic, important way.

"As soon as every tree is harvested, Mitch and I drive the baskets of olives to the oil pressing facility, about three hours away. This year, we got 110 bottles. It's beyond wonderful to give everyone a bottle of real honest-to-goodness olive oil that they had a hand in producing. With everyone working together to help make this product of nature, I can really feel the cycle from God to tree to table. These urban harvest parties open people's thinking to how much nature is right around us and what their own yards could be reimagined into."

Another neighbor, Janet, has a big old avocado tree in her backyard. She delivers bags of avocados to all the neighbors when they ripen. Hunting for them high in the tree with her tall fruit picker pole takes some doing, and sometimes friends come over to help. "People are so happy to get them every year," she said. "Avocados are like gold."

And our friend, Brad, in a completely different part of town, told me, "My piano teacher gave me a huge bag of Meyer lemons from his tree. Everyone likes marmalade on buttered toast. So I've just made fourteen jars of lemon marmalade to give to our friends and neighbors. I love to do it." I love that he does it too—and that so many neighbors recognize the bounty right in their own yards.

THANK
YOU!

And Olga, who'd made the chicken dinner for Leslie's family so long ago said, "My lemon tree puts out hundreds of lemons. Everyone around me gets a sack of lemons on their doorstep. I like to share the goodness that I have been blessed with and to see people's smiles when I ask if they want some."

I came home the other day to find so many different things neighbors had left on my doorstep—two empty vases, a couple of empty mason jars, some cleaned Tupperware and a bottle of rosé. What a funny yet warm welcome. The thrift store vases I'd given out to those nearby full of roses. The mason jars had gone out full of fresh-squeezed juice from our Valencia orange tree. The Tupperware went to a neighbor recovering from Covid and another recovering from a surgery with beef stew in it, and the wine had come back as a thanks from someone else but for what, I can't remember. These weren't prearranged trades. I looked at all the washed receptacles and almost laughed: Is this a new language for Covid times?

Noisy Neighbors, Darkened Blinds

What if you have truly difficult neighbors? Is there a way to love those neighbors as you love and even protect your family, yourself?

Marcie and Dan told me about their neighbors. "The whole family next door fought loud and partied loud," said Dan, "and the teenage son was so angry and surly whenever we saw him. We were civil with them—never friendly—but civil, even tried to say hi to the son but it was always met with anger. The music was an ongoing irritant, but we just lived with it, only asked them to keep it down when we had some kind of special occasion ourselves, and they would. We felt the parents were doing their best to keep their kids close, to make sure they partied at home, and the parents themselves had some problems too. What can we say? Our houses are close together."

Marcie continued the story. "But then we went through a true nightmare. Somebody came by and shot at their house. A drive-by shooting! This was enough for us to start thinking we had to move. Well, a few months later, the son was convicted of murder. We went through anger and sorrow and never knowing exactly what he'd done. He went to jail. Horrible as it was, we also felt relieved. There were still loud parties, but our fear after the shooting was gone. And gradually the other kids grew up, and soon it was mostly happy sounds, with the grandparents babysitting during the day.

"One day a few years ago," she said, "the mother came to the door. Her son's sentence, at seventeen, had been life without the possibility of parole. But now she was almost distraught with new hope. Would we please, please sign this petition to repeal the law that allowed minors to be sentenced for life? Would we please, please take it to church and ask people there to sign it as well? We still felt hurt and wary about all that had gone on but, in our eyes, this was an inhumane law. What seventeen-year-old cannot be rehabilitated? We put our personal feelings aside and helped with the petition. We never really did become friends, but after all that had happened over the years, for them and for us, we fell into easier exchanges, more familiarity, over the fence..."

❋

Jennifer said, "In my old neighborhood, one house was always dark with the blinds pulled down, but we knew Charles lived there. He'd lived there with his mother, and when she died, he kept on living there alone. He was about 50 and wore the most worn-out clothes. His T-shirts were grey and threadbare. I generally wave and say hello to everyone, but Charles didn't like it. It almost made him mad. One day, I was walking my dog and Charles came at me fast on his bike, almost like he wanted to run me over. I jumped out of the way and almost fell into the bushes. It scared me and you know, if you get scared, it scares your dog. My giant Newfoundland, Paris, bared her teeth and acted like she was going to bite him. Kind of almost did, but didn't. Well, two days later, I got a certified letter in my mailbox from Charles saying that he was going to sue us. My husband was so upset and wanted to get a lawyer right away, but I said, 'No. Wait, let me see if I can handle this.'

"I wrote Charles the best, nicest letter I could. I said, 'Please don't sue me. You scared me and that scared my dog. Really, she's never bitten anyone. I'm so sorry this happened and I really apologize. I realize how upset you are. Please accept my apology.' A couple of days go by, then there's a note in my mailbox from Charles. 'Okay. I won't,' is all it said. Isn't letting it go and doing some over-apologizing better than getting lawyers?

"I just felt that Charles really needed to be blessed. I started to pray for him, affirming how loved he was and how his beauty showed to all. I'd envision him full of love and light, you know, to lift his spirits. I did this every day for weeks. I'm a nut. But I love doing stuff like this. Every time I saw him on his bike, I waved like we were friends. I wouldn't just say hi, I'd say 'How far ya going today, Charles?' I'd tell him how great he looked. It embarrassed him, but he began to like it. He started answering me and we started having little conversations. Then one day, oh my gosh! Charles rode by and he had on new clothes! He'd bought new T-shirts and they were colorful! One day I saw a blue one, another day a green one. He was smiling, something he never, never, ever did before. I can't take credit, I don't. But it made me so happy."

❋

"It was a shock, moving to an unincorporated area," Anne said. "And I didn't know what a private road meant. What it means is you have to cooperate with everyone else on the road. The city and county don't take care of things, you and your neighbors have to. Well, one homeowner was kinda the king. He'd lived there the longest but actually he was a big bully and an alcoholic. It was painful and difficult dealing with him. He would do things like dump cement in the creek bed, and then Fish and Game would come after all of us. He'd go on about government regulations and he wasn't going to listen to anyone. But after some time, he moved! The vibe changed so much, and I started loving where I live. To know I could work together with my neighbors felt great.

"A new homeowner moved onto the road. He is from Iran. He and I had to talk about which trees had to be removed. We tried to work out the details through emails, and he seemed so harsh and abrupt. Mean, actually. My thought was, oh no, not another problem—we'll never agree on which trees have to be removed. But once we started walking the road together and discussing it, I realized that he was actually very nice—it's just that his written English was poor. Communicating only through emails was messing everything up."

Asked Bill to bring home two extra croissants from the bakery. Texted Jama and Joanne, next door, and told them to look on the wall for a little brown sack. Happy Sunday morning. It makes me happy to do something spontaneously, even though they may have had breakfast already; even though they may be avoiding gluten; even if they may come home in a week and find a bag full of ants, compliments of their stir-crazy neighbor. My spirits lift when I can reach beyond myself and my own. (p.s.—later a thank you text came in. Ants didn't get a chance.)

Oh—Those Bad Rays!

There is a black and white picture of myself with freshly chopped off bangs and two straight braids. I'm sitting on the picnic table on the back patio, wearing my favorite jeans and T-shirt, and my hands are resting on my knees. This picture has all the freshness that a little child can hold, and when I think back, I'm grateful to have been a little too young to be the actual troublemaker. Not exactly innocent, just not actively thinking up ways to kill Mrs. Kozlowski's flowers the way Jeff and Dan and their friends did.

A little bunch of us had decided that Mrs. Kozlowski was mean. I cannot recall why we may have thought that. Her scratchy voice? Her really thick glasses? Maybe because she yelled at us for sitting on the wall that divided our properties. One day, we had so much time on our hands, we decided to pay her back for being so mean. Dad had a walk-in tool shed filled with gardening and house-repair equipment. We got an old orange juice can and went in there to mix up something bad. We poured a bit of everything we could find into it—malathion, paint thinner, the stuff for the mosquito fogger. Then, to make sure it was completely toxic, Danny's friend Tommy opened his pants and peed into the concoction. "There. That'll do it," he said with certainty. We all agreed. That'll do it. We went to the wall and hurled this bomb of bad over and right into her sweet peas. Then we laughed and ran away. Oh, ha ha. The boys didn't seem at all contrite when they peeked over the wall daily to watch a patch of brown grow in her flower bed.

And there was the construction site. A new house was being built on another subdivided lot a couple of blocks away. We were told again and again to leave that place alone, don't go there. So of course we'd sneak in after the workers left. We'd race around the open framework of the house-to-be—chasing each other up the roughed-out staircase, jumping from the plywood flooring into the mud around the newly poured foundation, leaping across the gaps in the sub flooring. All the while, we'd tell each other a well-known, unverified true story that went like this:

> A little boy was playing around in an unfinished house, a place he wasn't supposed to go to. He just loved wearing his cowboy hat, and this one time when he jumped from an unfinished step to the main floor—*here we'd jump from an unfinished step*—the string of his cowboy hat got caught on a big nail and—and... *hanged him!*

We repeated this tale endlessly as we played under the giant "No Trespassing" sign. Then, because we could, we'd horse around with all the surveying sticks that were set in the yard to mark off the garage-to-be oh, ha ha. Ha. . . what shall we do next?

Well, years and years later, more than fifty in fact, Bill and I found ourselves paying to tour the old Van Der Kar house. We love home tours. I'd have a chance to see the wonderful old place again, just a block from my childhood home on Santa Rosa. We kids had dug foxholes all over their yard for our big games of War. We'd dig them out of view of the kitchen window so Mrs. Van Der Kar wouldn't see us. That game went on for almost a year. Mary and Scottie Van Der Kar raised pigeons in a coop by the garage. I loved those pigeons. This beautiful old stone house had been the carriage house to a Victorian mansion next to it. It had been torn down while we were still children to build our new library. So many neighbors stood around watching it get torn down. Kevin and I stood in the gutters, leaning against the cool granite boulders, sharing a box of Milk Duds as the wrecking ball just whacked the old Col. Green mansion to smithereens. Kaboom! went the upper story with its Tiffany windows. Crash! went the mahogany balustrades—now the foyer was ripped open and Kevin said, "See those brass things dangling in there by a wire?" "Yeah," I said. "That's what they used for light before there was electricity." "That is so neat," I said. "Don't they want to save some of that stuff?"

To my surprise, the lady at the tour welcome table was none other than the big sister of our childhood playmates. Back then, Brooke Van Der Kar was the teenage sister we never saw, but when I realized who she was, I exclaimed, "Oh my gosh! I'm Mary Lea, Mary Lea Ray." At which point she retorted, "Oh—you mean one of the *bad* Rays?"

NO TRESPASSING

Bill burst out laughing. I laughed, she laughed, but I was also shaking my head. "How in the world are your brothers and sisters?" Brooke asked. The line to enter her home was forming behind us, but Brooke and I were locked in a time warp.

"Everybody's good," I said. "I'm a grandmother now." Then I recounted updates about those she would remember: "Dan's in real estate. Jeff was a high school theater teacher, but he passed away twenty years ago. Kevin's good, he's a florist. Johnny—" I slowed down. She nodded, "We all heard about that when it happened," Brooke said. I nodded slowly. "Yeah. So, Beth's a retired scientist," I continued. "Mark, the baby, he's a mortgage broker up in Sacramento." I pantomimed a sigh of relief. "We all turned out okay!" Brooke and I were smiling across all the years to one another.

"Mom thought you kids were such a pain!" Brooke said. I nodded, unable to disagree.

Seeing Brooke brought up so many memories of my brother John and his great friend, Tom Clemmens. How strange it was to see Tom's name etched into the sidewalk right around the corner when Bill and I moved into our big house thirty years ago. Tom must have put his name in the wet cement when no one was looking; he'd grown up nearby. He was in the car with my brother John the night John's jeep ran off the road. It was dark, and they were driving through the boonies of Nevada on their way to a bluegrass concert, and I don't know, they somehow ran off the road. John was thrown from the car and hit his head on a rock. He hung on for two weeks but then, died. And his friend, Tom? He was unhurt.

We'd never had this kind of sudden loss. Mom instantly looked so small and weary. I don't remember Dad saying a word, not one word to anyone. . . It makes me think, and what about the one million Americans who've just died in the pandemic? What anguish within their families, as was in ours for John.

All the neighbors got a kick out of John because right when he turned 16, he'd gone out and found a mailman delivery cart, bought it, got it home, worked on it for months in the driveway, and then drove it around. When he got it into really good shape, he took it all the way to the beach. On the freeways? Of course not, but taking city streets for hours all the way across LA to Santa Monica.

We might've been the *bad* Rays, but to be fair to my parents, nothing in their young lives prepared them for us. Mom was the only child of Ruthie and Jim. Ruthie used to keep Mom out of school so she could have company while Jim was on the road selling something or chasing some sure bet somewhere. As a little girl, all through the Roaring '20s, Mom was indulged with money they didn't have. When she should have been in school, she was on a cruise through the Panama Canal with Ruthie or, riding with Ruthie and the chauffeur around Manhattan looking for her father: what bar was he holding court in, cooking up some new business scheme. Mom witnessed so many screaming matches between her parents as Ruthie tried to shout some reality into Jim's dreaming brain. And when the money problems got really bad, Ruthie took herself back to work, this time as a photo model for *True Confessions*, a racy scandal and romance magazine. Mom didn't have a lot to go on in Ruthie for being a kind, consistent, loving-mother role model.

Dad grew up in almost-rural Illinois. All through elementary school, he was up early to go into the fields and check his traps for beaver and mink. That's how he made money. Shortly after high school graduation he waved goodbye to his mom and dad and hitchhiked to California. In 1933, there was a lot more going on in sun-drenched LA than in Wheaton. He did what he could to find his way, selling Fuller brushes and other stuff until the engines of World War II started turning over. Dad never had more than a high school education but he was full of quiet, methodical abilities so he went up the ladder at McDonnell Douglas, the company that built war planes. This meant he never got drafted—he was doing his part for the war by running the wing division, in charge of 2,500 workers. When he met and married Mom, who by then lived in Altadena with Ruthie and Jim, he thought his life would continue to be grand like that from then on—having plenty of money and taking Mom dancing to big band night clubs— but the war ended. They didn't need anyone to be in charge of the wing division for war planes anymore. So, he worked here and there in aerospace, owned a car wash, suffered a bankruptcy, worked as a contracts manager for construction companies, had bouts of unemployment, and ruined his health worrying about money. And, he raised all nine of us. So he was not amused by his son Jeff hollering out, "All you care about is that green stuff—money!" when they fought after Jeff got arrested for protesting and wearing the American flag as a poncho. But Jeff went on to use that bravado to become an adored high school teacher; so much so that when he died, former students flew from across the country to be at his funeral.

My sister Sally was four years older than me, and Mom's right hand. She started changing diapers when she was seven. She helped Mom with dinner every night. She made sure we littler ones did our jobs. One time, at age eleven, she watched all of us while Mom and Dad took a weekend for themselves. Jimmy was almost fifteen, but they put Sally in charge, knowing Jimmy would have ducked out of there as soon as they drove off. And too, Ruthie was just a garden walk away. When Ruthie came in on Saturday morning to check on us, eleven-year-old Sally was making a big pan of scrambled eggs, and Ruthie announced, "Those are the worst-looking *pancakes* I ever saw." Sally looked at her. "Ruthie. They're eggs!" But Ruthie stared at them, unconvinced. She had to get a spoon and check for herself. So, really, Sally was in charge.

Sally loved having secret boyfriends that necessitated her sneaking out of the house. We shared a bedroom and I heard her endless plans to run away the second she turned 18, to a place where nobody could tell her what to do. I was expecting something awful to happen on that long-awaited birthday but, Mom baked a cake, we had a nice dinner and—funny—Sally suddenly lost interest in her schemes. But she did grow up fast to get herself out of the house and away from being Mom's right hand—only to start her own big family. The two children from her husband's first marriage, and the four they had together—Sally raised them all into a fun-loving crowd of productive adults who loved her and love one another. Sally was the only one of my sibs who simply could not quit smoking. At age 67, when she was diagnosed with lung cancer and given a matter of months, she said, "Please—do not feel sorry for me! I am the luckiest person I know." Few people would be able to say something like that at such a time. Her acceptance is one of the biggest gifts she ever gave me.

I don't know. . . all told, and sparing poor Mrs. Kozlowski, I guess I'll take our Ray brand of bad.

The Deliciousness of Pie

A street not far from mine seems to have everything. The sloping yards barely have any fencing between them. A few majestic sycamores hang shaggy branches across the view of the mountains, and at the end of the street is a public golf course that appears like an endless meadow. The neighbors know and like one another.

But then, Boston Street has always been exceptionally friendly, even way back when several of my mother's friends lived there. These women formed themselves into a fun-loving group called the Boston Street Sherry Club. The club's main activity was the enjoyment of sherry and food items that go with sherry, as well as conversation that is accompanied by, yes, more sherry. Many a Friday afternoon was spent deep into club business, which produced things like multi-family beach vacations or group classes in reupholstering couches.

When Bill and I returned to the area in the '80s, somebody said we should check out the 4th of July parade on Boston Street. For a two-block stretch, all the neighbors were out, and little kids festooned in 4th of July finery paraded on bikes and trikes. Leading this darling, motley parade was a dad in a Honda hatchback. A boom box taped to the roof sprayed out Motown tunes like a moving lawn sprinkler. Neighbors were laughing and sharing food, sprawled on lawns and curbs. I seldom experience jealousy, but I was jealous out of my mind! How could so many fun people live on one street! How did it get like that?

Today, I myself have a few friends on Boston Street: Jane and Lu and Peggy. They, and a few of us other gal-pals, have happy hour many a Friday afternoon. I wanted to know how, exactly, they'd met one another. The three of them laughed.

"Remember, Lu, it was Thanksgiving," Jane began.

Lu nodded. "We were already living there a few years, but we worked all the time and weren't around," she said.

Jane continued her side of the story. "I had all these people coming. The turkey was in the oven, and halfway through, the oven breaks. Or just stops. I got out the hot mitts and my husband, Rod, and I walked that turkey across the street at 3 p.m. and knocked on the door. Our first hello was followed by— '*and do you have room in your oven?*'" (And there was room, because Lu and Jay barbecue theirs.)

Then Lu corrected Jane. "No Jane, actually, the first time we met was when I saw you trying to carry one of your 70-pound dogs home in your arms. I told Jay to go help that poor woman!"

Again, Jane laughed. "That dog was trying to run away back to San Diego, where I'd gotten him from a rescue." The three neighbors paused to nod and remember.

Peggy chimed in, "We moved onto Boston Street two days before I gave birth." Everyone remembered. They'd each been in their homes long enough to see all the kids on the street grow up and leave. "We're the ones who sort of watch out for the block now," Jane said. "Rod and I and Jay and Lu bring a pie to everyone who moves in."

"We want newcomers to love the street as much as we do," Lu said.

The idea of presenting new neighbors with a pie. . . I had only done it once. Thought about doing it a million times, because when we moved into our big house, the neighbors across the street came over with a homemade flan to welcome us. But by the time I did bring a new neighbor a pie, they'd already been here five years. Also, shoot, it was a frozen one.

St. Therese of Lisieux was known for doing the tiniest of acts—like, say sweeping a porch or greeting passersby—but she did it with so much intention that they became elevated far above what the small acts actually were. When a chance arises it is a delicate thing, because that chance will pass—and there really is only the narrow window of *now,* right now, to be the person who does the things you wished you would do.

That jealousy-creating 4th of July long ago on Boston Street? When our kids were three and seven and nine, that Summer was the now, right now, to act on what had been in my mind. I didn't know a dad with a hatchback, but I wrote a little skit about the midnight ride of Paul Revere.

Other parents jumped in to help. One little girl appeared in a spray-painted hooped sheet as the Liberty Bell, another as Sojourner Truth. A seven-year-old performed as Paul Revere himself, calling out, "The Bwittish are coming! The Bwittish are coming!" Twenty-five people brought beach chairs to our front lawn to watch their children come from behind a little curtain in capes and costumes. I can still remember the satisfaction of fantasizing about doing something and then actually doing it. Of bringing the *maybe* into the now. And after the show, there was pie for all.

That is how our neighborhood 4th of July began. The little skit dropped out but the following year, the costumes came back in a funny little kid's parade. The dads came out with their grills so everybody could enjoy hamburgers and hotdogs in the street, under the camphor trees. The following year, we got the fire department to come— with their hoses! There was no controlling it now. Each year it grew. Water balloons. Three legged races. Raffle tickets— with our neighbor, Sherry, always a big winner (How many tickets could she buy?). Mitch has worked the hotdog and hamburger grill for years but everything's been cancelled during the lockdown. "It's funny," he said as we chatted by phone, "our neighbors are so proud of our 4th of July event that they invite their friends, so there's lots of people we don't actually know. But the more the merrier. I know of a couple who actually moved here just because of our 4th of July. I hope next year we can start it up again. . ."

One of my problems is that I have way too many thoughts at a time. Too many racing thoughts. Too many competing ideas at one time. I want to work on mindfulness. So, working on mindfulness is on my pandemic checklist. Because how can anyone be present to a place or a person who might be standing right in front of them if their mind is so filled up and busy? Today, I'm trying a technique— they say it's really good. It's to take a walk slowly, very slowly, for twenty minutes and try to notice as much of everything as you can: people—dogs—cars—mailboxes—the sun shining. . . clouds. Just to notice and to take in. They say it expands your time and calms your mind.

I headed out onto the sidewalk, eager to get going with my mindfulness. Well, there were plenty of cars and the sun was shining, but going slowly was difficult. Not fun. The urge to just get on with it, and then get home to make some calls, was powerful. I devolved into repeating the phrase, "Do less and live more, do less and live more." After what seemed like two hours, the twenty-minute walk was over. I'll try again tomorrow.

Gentler Gifts

We have had a few people who just by their presence have made our neighborhood unique. One was Little Cathy. Cathy lived around the corner from Bill and me, and she became more and more bent over as she worked the sidewalks with her red wagon, picking up plastic and cans, never scavenging from private trash cans, but picking things up from the gutters to recycle. Various people had various things to say about her: her parents babied her so much she never grew up, and she's looked down all her life so now she actually can't lift her head all the way up. I didn't feel comfortable saying hello to her, but then a neighbor friend said, "Oh no, she mows my lawn." Another neighbor friend said, "Oh no, she feeds our cats." So I changed from fearful to curious and began waving to her as I drove by. Seems like I saw her every day.

Little Cathy and her disabled brother would sit on their porch in metal rockers when she wasn't out collecting cans and bottles and watch the world go by. This was the house they'd grown up in, the house their parents had died in. The house they were normal little children in, before life unfolded as it does for each of us and she became strange and he became wheelchair bound.

Little Cathy never looked dirty, but she never wore anything but baggy jeans, an old T-shirt, a canvas bucket hat, and a plaid man's shirt. Her straight red hair went grey over the years, and she got skinnier and skinnier. When I heard people were leaving little sacks of food on her doorstep, I started doing it too—not really groceries, more like sandwiches and oatmeal cups. She said she didn't cook because her stove was broken. Cathy didn't want people to come inside, their little peeling white house was chock full of their parent's things and the things from their childhood. But if you took the time, Cathy could overcome her shyness and talk intelligently about recycling. It was true, she didn't really ever look up. For six blocks around, you could see her scouting for recyclables, perhaps talking to someone if they'd been patient enough to make a bridge with her.

❋

Sherry told me about her neighbor John. "John lived next door," Sherry said. "He was extremely old. I always looked to see if his newspaper was taken in. We'd chat if he was out watering. As he got even older, John took to wandering up and down the street in his pajamas, and I'd run out and redirect him, get him back to his door safely. His daughter lived far away but I started calling her to give reports on how he was doing. Whenever she came into town, she always stopped in to see me and thank me. Since I could see his front door from my home office, I was the only one who could know exactly how he was doing. She was so thankful for this. Every single year we received a Christmas card from John with a long and very thoughtful message. It always delighted me that it was stamped and sent through the post, all the way from next door."

❋

Another friend, Mel, told me, "Some people can't let go of stuff, and the lady next door was in way over her head, her yard was an overgrown junkyard disaster, could barely see the house. But she was sweet, and her adult daughter, who lived with her, had special needs. When she was out trying to put a little water on the dead shrubs, or tidy the boxes of newspapers on her porch, she would tell me how worried she was about how messy her house and yard were. I just decided, yes, I could do this, and started paying my gardeners to do her yard as well."

❋

"There she is!" Janet announced excitedly as we drove past a house near hers. "Who?" I asked. "Grace!" Janet pointed to a lady so old she looked see-through. Old Grace stood in the middle of her lawn with a running hose in her hand. Grace smiled at us, but waving required too much effort. Janet pointed out Grace's attire, her thing about color. "It must be blue day," Janet said, with a big smile in her voice. "See—everything she's wearing is blue." Sure enough, Grace wore blue pull-on pants. A blue cotton shirt. A blue sweater and a blue chiffon scarf around her neck. Her shoes were blue, too. "Oh, my word!" I said.

"Don't you know Grace?" Janet asked.

"No. I'm three blocks away. I've never noticed her before."

But after that, like others, I started seeing Yellow Grace waiting on the lawn for a ride. Or maybe, when she was up to it, I'd spy Green Grace a bit down her block, admiring a cat. Pink Grace might be smelling a rose, on another block. "She often makes it by my house, and we will chat as I'm weeding," Janet said as we continued on our way. "She looks amazing on purple days. I want to be like that when I get really, really old." She laughed, like it was a joke, but then again, I know Janet . . .

Soon Janet was telling me about a time when Grace still rode the bus and went places with her walker. Janet had fallen in to walk beside her and asked where she was off to. "To her button club!" Janet said. "And she pulled out a little paper of beautiful buttons. She would get together with friends to show off or trade buttons they had!"

Grace got even older and took a turn for the worse. She'd sit by her open door, a blanket over her lap and a caretaker next to her. The caretaker wasn't dressing Grace the way she'd always liked. Also, the lawn was dying. Then Grace herself died. Her house went on the market, and the new people couldn't wait to paint and remodel everything. Maybe some of us will come to know them but, in the meantime, Grace is missed.

Today, I saw a little lady standing on my corner, and fifteen minutes later she was still standing there. I walked down to see if she was lost. She said she had called the senior ride van to pick her up to go shopping and it was supposed to have arrived 30 minutes ago. Oh, the poor lady I thought—but yikes! Am I the one? Do I have to stop what I'm doing and give her a ride? "Hmm. Hmm," I said, trying to find a way out of it. "Where do you need to go?" Shoot, only a few miles away. But hold on, I told myself—maybe I'm being given an opportunity. Maybe even a test. Am I not trying to grow? "Wait here a minute. I'll go get my car," I said. Taking her where she needed to go probably took an hour, all totaled. Once I'd given myself permission to move off my schedule, this little task was not as frustrating as I thought it would be. No, quite the opposite. I felt energized all day.

The Business of Childhood

I glanced out the window to watch the little kids next door setting up a lemonade stand. Some things never change. They had a card table, a sign, their paper cups, and a big pitcher of summer in a cup, the lemonade itself. Ella and Graham commenced calling out to cars as they passed... Ah, I hope everyone gets to have the summer of their lemonade stand.

When my friends and younger siblings and I were still well under ten years old, we spent lots of time in the yard of the mystery lady, Mrs. Randstrum, two doors down. Her house had low, dark-green eaves, and her yard was full of chrysanthemums and dahlias and hydrangeas. We kids could see her out in her flowered dress and apron working in her flower beds but we never spoke to her or ever really saw her face. We'd watch for her to drive off somewhere and then sneak into her yard. We carefully skirted her flower beds so she'd never suspect we were there. She had a little pond tucked back into the bushes that teemed with guppies. We'd bring jars with us and catch a bunch of them and take them home as our new pets. July and August were such hot and smoggy months, and we'd tuck ourselves into her bushes by the pond, where it was so cool and calming.

Sometimes we just waved our hands around in the pungent green water and let the guppies swim between our fingers. I loved those little fishes.

During the summer of our lemonade stand, a great idea came to me: Why not sell guppies right alongside cups of lemonade! Barbara's brother, Tom, made lots of money selling his hamsters. Shoot, he got a quarter apiece for them. Surely people would pay five cents for a living fish if they were willing to pay five cents for a cup of lemonade. And we always needed money to keep up the supplies for our club. There were four of us in our current club: me, my brother Kevin, and Maya and Eric. Sometimes we liked to hold club meetings in Mrs. Randstrum's bushes. The main purpose for the club was to figure out what game to play next and to have a reason to eat candy. Meetings always began with one of us opening a box of Jello and passing it around. We would dip our index finger into the powder and then lick off the sugary deliciousness.

So I caught about thirty of the dear little guppies and carried them in a big jar to the lemonade stand, which for the past week had been a going operation. I was the only one on duty at the stand that day. I set up ten paper cups of water with one guppy in each and started calling out, "Guppies! Guppies for sale!" In retrospect, I should have made a sign that said "Guppies." Before long, a man came jogging up Santa Rosa. He was officially the first jogger I had ever seen—a man out running for no reason in shorts and an undershirt. No one back then exercised in public.

LEMONADE
5¢

He came sweating and panting up to my stand and said, “I’ll have a cup.” He put a nickel on the table and without looking—and before I could stop him—picked up a paper cup and gulped down—no, not lemonade! A guppy. I cried out, “No!” as the tiny fish just went down his throat. His eyes bugged out and his hand flew to his mouth. He dropped his cup on the street, said something bad under his breath, and bolted on. I quickly poured all the little guppies back into the big jar where they were safe. How could I have let this happen? Truly horrified, I walked the big jar back to the pond and let them go.

The summer before, Jeff, Dan, Kevin, and I set up our lemonade stand at the end of the driveway. Mom said, “I’ll buy four cans of lemonade to get you started. After that, you’ll have to get your own supplies out of your earnings.” We pulled all the necessities together—a card table, a sign, paper cups and a big pitcher of lemonade. We got right down to business yelling, jumping up and down, and waving our arms at each car that passed our corner. This alarmed drivers. They swerved away, afraid they’d just hit a kid, and sped off mad. “No playing in the streets!” they’d shout. But then a friend of Mom’s would drive by and hand us fifty cents and say, “You kids drink it,” and then drive on. We would—we’d gulp down ten cups of lemonade because that’s what fifty cents would buy. Being good at business meant we wouldn’t drink a drop more than was paid for.

We worked that stand every day from noon to four. But before long, Carl and Big Scottie got jealous. They lived across the street, and they set up their own stand right across from ours. "Not fair! Go somewhere else!" we yelled at them. "It's a free country," they yelled back. Also, not fair that they had a lemon tree and didn't have to buy lemonade, so they could afford bigger cups. Our customers started going over there. That's when Jeff said, "Let's sell candy too."

So we walked to Thrifty's and bought a few dollars' worth of candy bars: Snickers, Hershey's, Red Hots, Pay Days. Candy bars were five cents then. Lemonade *and* candy! Lemonade *and* candy! We were making so much money that our business practices became lax and we started eating the candy, but this is what we did: We'd taunt Carl and Big Scottie by going dangerously near their stand, very slowly unwrapping a Snickers, and eating it right in front of them.

Don't get me wrong, Jeff and Dan could be awful, but Carl threw the first rock. Instantly, Jeff and Dan threw rocks right back and then rushed them—pushed their stand right over, spilling everything. So Carl and Big Scottie rushed them right back, chasing them across the street, yelling "Get 'em! Get 'em!" and knocking our table over, spilling everything. The boys fell on each other, punching and hitting one another. Kevin and I ran away to get Mom. The yelling brought Susan and Barbara out of Susan's house. They started yelling because of all the excitement. Mom came out, yelling. She got right in there, slapping the pile of boys apart from one another. "That's it! That's it! You're all done! The lemonade stands are closed! Closed! Clean up this street!" Everyone stood frozen for a minute, too worked up to respond. "Move!" Mom commanded.

At this moment, Ruthie rounded the corner, home early from the races. She wanted to pull into the driveway. This galvanized us to move the wrecked stuff out of the way. To Mom, Ruthie said, "What's going on, Jane?" "Business disputes," Mom said, as if that explained how mad the boys had gotten with one another. Ruthie, having missed the fight, commented cheerfully, "Be careful, boys, or you'll end up in Sing Sing. Who wants to know how I did today? Came home early!" Ruthie had that sparkle in her eye that meant she'd really won. She got out of the car, and Susan, Barbara, Carl, Big Scottie, Kevin, Jeff, Dan, and I watched as she headed toward our house. "Well, come on," she said. We followed her twinkling charms to where she'd settled herself on the front porch. She opened her pocketbook and said, "Seems like you kids don't deserve this, but here you go." And she handed each of us a whole dollar bill. We all looked down—amazed, thrilled, unworthy.

Once Mom and Ruthie were in the kitchen, Mom said, "Mother! Why did you do that?" Ruthie gave a little wave of her hand. "They'll remember it," she said, and began preparing her gimlet.

During clean up, we retrieved from the gutter as many candy bars as we could. Carl and Big Scottie cleaned up their stuff. The boys all looked at one another with miserable expressions. It seemed like they wanted to say something, but they didn't, or couldn't.

Today, my heart felt heavy and worried with world news, the virus, politics—was a war brewing?—oh when will it all get better? Anyway, the day was empty enough to take myself off to an outdoor exhibition on our local wildlife. We live so close to the mountains. Maybe looking at a stuffed mountain lion and beautiful photography would help my mood. . .What did help were all the quotes incorporated into the exhibits from Jane Goodall. One great one was, "We have so far to go to realize our human potential for compassion, altruism, and love." It struck me because I'm used to thinking about human potential as learning, achieving and creating concrete skills, not nurturing inward qualities— which we all have. Goodall's point is that these are the new concrete skills we need to save our world. But the quote that did me the most good that day was: "Hope does not deny the evil, but is a response to it." Thank you, Jane Goodall.

Beyond Your Own Backyard

Today was the day to call my longtime friend Michele and invite her over. She'd been a high school friend of Jeff's. Together, they fully lived the colorful '60s. Though Jeff has been gone for twenty years, the memories they'd shared of getting arrested, of hitchhiking, of sleeping in pads of friends of friends, of doing so many things they ought to've regretted but just didn't, are legend. Michele and I became friends in what I think back on as the Peter Pan days of my twenties, when a bunch of us were neighbors in a bungalow court in Pasadena. Typically, bungalow courts have a dozen or so tiny cottages or bungalow-homes situated around a courtyard in a garden setting. It was a mode of balmy California living popular in the early 1900s. California, the land of milk and honey. Our court, Reinway, was so companionable. There were always offers for dinner, instant parties, constant ins and outs of one another's homes. No one who lived in Reinway Court has ever completely shaken off those easygoing days.

Michele and I greeted each other at six feet apart and settled ourselves on the front porch, calculating how much air flow was between us. . . It was January 2021, cases of the virus were soaring after the Christmas season, and no vaccine yet. How had life changed so swiftly? Is a global catastrophe always right around the corner on any given day? Could it be we just don't realize it because most of the time we're actually very, very lucky?

Our front porch offers a perfect view of the birds in the gingko tree and the goings-on of the street. By spending time in the front yard, I've made friends with the gentle mourning doves who walk around in the bushes, as well as the playful phoebes and the towhees. Towhees are so intent on bugs in the grass that they'll walk right past my foot.

It was cold, so I offered Michele a late-afternoon lemon hot toddy (homemade lemonade heated with a generous splash of Tennessee honey whisky) poured into big green mugs. Umm, we said in unison.

Today, I wanted to hear why Michele had worked so hard to get a trashy corner near her house cleaned and beautified. With her, the Mr. Rogers quote comes to mind: "I hope you're proud of yourself for all the times you've said 'yes', when all it meant was extra work for you and was seemingly helpful only to somebody else."

"It's so satisfying being able to make things happen," she said cheerfully. "And I really care." This simple phrase struck me. *I really care. I really care.* Some people care—not just about their own house and home, but about the town their house sits in. They want our common spaces to be beautiful. They want government, infrastructure, all the institutions to work well. We all want that, but most of us hope someone else will do the work so we can continue along unhampered.

"And you know me," she continued. "I've always liked knowing what's going on and being a part of the community. But the real thing is that when Mark and I lived in Thailand for those ten years, we realized how lucky we are here. Over there, an ordinary person can't do anything about a bad situation. Absolutely nothing!"

"What do you mean?" I asked. Rolling her eyes, she swiftly counted off on her fingers – "Rabid dogs running around. *Open* sewers! Having to wait 40 minutes at a traffic light. Can you imagine the frustration of waiting 40 minutes for the light to change? People routinely broke their legs in potholes, which were everywhere. Living in Bangkok, there was nothing I, as an individual, could do about any of that. So Mark and I decided if we ever came back to the States, we were going to be better citizens. That we wouldn't take things for granted.

"These days," Michele continued, "people have big private lives but small neighborhood or civic lives. For me, I'd drive by this eyesore by my house every day, and every day I'd think how nice that ratty piece of dusty corner could look if it were landscaped. How pretty it might become if people cared. Sometimes, it's a lot easier than you may think to make a big change in your town. In Altadena," she said with a chuckle, "it only takes about 20 votes to get onto the town council." Today that trashy, ratty corner has a bench, a few young oak trees, a granite marker, and blooming native plants.

We paused in our conversation to take in the cold light of the afternoon and sip our hot toddies. "But you know, I learned from my mother," Michele mused. I remember Michele's mother, Kit, a white haired and bright, feisty little woman from Wales. "She was always doing something: PTA president or getting behind town issues when they came along. I remember being five years old and going with her on all her volunteering." The picture of this made me smile. My dynamic friend as a small child, tagging along as her mother, an immigrant war bride to this country, made her way in her new country by doing volunteer work. Are our children today tagging along with their parents to learn how things get done? Amazing to think that experiences at five or six can teach us how to be excellent citizens, even though we might not act on this for many years into the future.

Wrote a note of thanks to Armando, our mailman, and left it for him in the box. He was gone awhile but now he's back. He'd been hit by a car. I am grateful to know Armando's name. All these years, if he'd just been "the mailman," I might not have known to wish him godspeed in his recovery. I might not have been as glad to see him on the sidewalk. Without knowing his name, he would have stayed just the mailman, instead of Armando, the generous guy who comes by every day.

Raining Kittens

I secretly liked that at one point our neighborhood was full of—overrun with, some would say—feral cats. Coyotes hadn't invaded yet, and I used to enjoy seeing a cat just strolling across the street, happy as you please. We also had Popsicle, an orange and white tabby, who was our local personality. Popsicle never met an open door he didn't enter. He took his naps in comfy porch chairs anywhere around the neighborhood. He even got himself all the way to St. Elizabeth's elementary school and, taking himself into the principal's office, curled up in her chair.

Today, I wanted to take another stroll with Jan and finish the conversation we had started a few months ago when she, Tom and I walked to the little garden. It was a fine late afternoon and I headed down to her end of the street. Our sidewalks can be so beautiful, dappled in shade and edged with shrubs on one side, a grass strip to the curb on the other. *How long will there be enough water to keep everything so deeply beautifully green*, I wondered. Some people say not long, not long at all.

We met up in front of her place. Jan and Tom have already taken their lawn out and redone it with drought-tolerant succulents and colorful pots.

With a warm greeting, Jan said, "You wanted to hear about the cats?" I nodded. We fell into walking side by side. "Those kitties brought a bunch of us together, down on our block. Before the cat dilemma—which went on for months—we'd entered a period when we'd all gotten busy and just didn't have that much contact."

"Everyone gets busy into their own worlds," I acknowledged.

"But then it started," Jan continued, "when my neighbor, a few doors down, came home and found two tiny kittens struggling out from under her barbecue cover and mewing across her driveway."

"Really? How in the world?" I said, suddenly thinking of an equally improbable time when I was little and playing in my school friend Kay's yard, not far from here. I looked up into the tree and saw an honest-to-goodness anteater climbing around up there. We called out to her mother. Her mother called the neighbors. The neighbors called their neighbors and—guess what? The man who lived behind them really had an anteater as a pet and it'd escaped. If that could happen, I guess kittens can come out from a barbecue.

"My neighbor called me over," said Jan. "Oh no. Oh no. What the heck? Where was mama? Where were the others? These little kittens had just been born. But we couldn't find where in the world the others were or who the mama-cat was. It took her several hours, but through the NextDoor app she found someone willing to bottle feed the two orphans. Much later that day, we spied mama-kitty carrying her other kittens one by one across Catalina Street to Nohemi's yard. So she and I went over, Nohemi joined the hunt, and the three of us looked and looked. We couldn't find where mama had hidden them. Not in the basement, not in the bushes, not under the cars. We searched for mama-kitty every day and talked about her every day. I don't know where we found the time, because we spent so much of it on the mystery of these kittens."

As Jan told her tale, we passed house after house built in earlier eras, each with their hundred-year-old street trees standing by, the wonderful camphors, the tree-spirits. . . House and tree, tree and house holding everything in place.

When Tom and Jan bought their house it was in a falling-down condition. Many of us watched as they turned it into a work of art. Not only did they do things like install porch lights made of beautiful art glass, but they found some special product and painstakingly removed all the texture-coating from the redwood siding of their Craftsman home, on all four sides of the house. It took months. It inspired many of us to up the attention to our own houses.

"Then one day—there she was!" Jan continued, "But now mama-kitty was moving her kittens *back* across Catalina Street and then across Topeka to Lorenzo's yard. We watched them popping in and out of Lorenzo's bushes for the next couple of weeks. All of us neighbors had such fun watching them play, but they were way too quick to catch. Having this little shared experience was so good for us in being able to connect with one another again." I nodded in agreement as we peacefully strolled down the middle of the street. Traffic is a fraction of what it used to be before the lockdown.

"Before long, oh no! Mama-kitty's pregnant again." We both laughed. "And Lorenzo's yard, for whatever reason, didn't suit her because now they were in *my* yard, blending in with our two cats. Very pregnant mama-kitty disappeared for a couple of days. But then there she was, all proud, with her new bunch, carrying them one by one from—yes—Nohemi's yard, *back* to Lorenzo's *again.* Five more kittens! The old kittens in our yard, the new ones in Lorenzo's yard. And pretty soon all of them were back in our yard! We were crawling with cats.

"Have you ever tried to catch a wild cat? Mostly our attempts ended up in laughter and we'd leave it with, 'Let's try again tomorrow.' Then a neighbor on NextDoor called out—*what's with all the feral cats?* I private messaged him, hoping he wouldn't be mad at me, and to tell him how we four neighbors were watching out for them and yes, yes, I knew it looked really bad, all these community cats living on our porch. I thought he was going to be a problem, but no! This fellow from three blocks away turned out to really love cats and offered to come over with some friends and help us catch them all. He brought humane cages and everything. It took us all one entire Saturday, but we finally caught 'em all. Then *he* took all these kittens, nine of them, to the set of the soap opera he worked on. That whole motley crew of kittens got adopted by the actors and the cameramen and the assistants. It worked out perfectly. We all still laugh about it and a new period of cooperating for us, I think, was because of those wild cats."

We finally started having our monthly coffee group again after untold months of Covid separation. We met outside, on my back patio, this group of women who've been friends a long, long time. Many of us lived in Reinway Court and here we are, still friends forty years later!

I posed a question: "When was a time you had a lovely, positive experience with a neighbor?" Coffee cups paused—then a burst of talk. "Remember how Joan SLAMMED that door as you passed her place?" Elaine blurted. "And Eric calling the cops on the kids over the fence!" Michele laughed. "Allen sneaking around," Cynthia began. "Wait!" I called out to the table. "Positive, I'm looking for positive!" The entire table fell stone silent. Hmm, hmm— then a barrage of laughing. "It's too hard!" they mocked, good naturedly. "Positive?! Oh come-on!"

Mrs. McKay

There'd always been rumors about a witch, or possibly just a crabby old lady, who lived on the overgrown five-acre parcel around the corner from us when we were kids. A giant old house sat at the top of the long, winding driveway. Rumors said she kept all kinds of animals. We'd never seen her, but we knew she was up there. Mom and Dad's friends would say things like, "She's a regular kook," and "Where's the health department when you want them?" Rumor said she raised the animals for science experiments, or maybe it was to feed starving children in Africa. Or, no, maybe it was that she collected old, retired movie-star animals. Well, one hot summer day when Susan wasn't around and Barbara wasn't around and Janine's mother said no one could come over, Kevin and I, age ten and eleven, decided to dare each other to go up Mrs. McKay's driveway and see for ourselves what was up there.

As we approached the shingled, old house we heard a harsh, "Hey, kids! What do you want?" Stepping from the bushes was an old lady with red hair. She wore red stretch pants, and her gnarled toes poked out from worn red tennis shoes. Pieces of horsehair sprang from the corners of her glasses where she'd fixed them. "What *do* you want?" she repeated. She eyed us sharply.

"We—ah, we heard there were animals here," I managed to say.

"You can't come trespassing here," she answered. We turned to hurry away, but then she looked us over, "Unless," she said, as we turned back around, "you want to work. Do you know how to work?" We nodded our heads in unison. "Do you have any animals at home?" she interrogated.

Kevin managed to croak, "I have a guppy." I managed to say, "I have a hamster."

Mrs. McKay rolled her eyes. "Well, if you want to stay you have to work. Kids don't loiter here. Do you want to work?" We nodded again. "All right then—but I'll be watching you. Go down the path there, past the monkeys and the guinea pigs, find the other kids and help 'em bury the dead pony." Electricity ran through us. *A dead pony?*

As if hypnotized, we did as she commanded. Not *only* did we pass the cage of monkeys and the row of guinea pig cages, but goat pens, a row of kennels populated with only bulldogs, a flock of chickens, geese, and ducks, and the pony pen. Past this, under a pepper tree, we found four kids we'd never met before. They were digging a great big hole, and beside the hole lay a real live dead pony. "More help!" they all seemed to cry out together when they saw us.

It's funny, from that exact moment on, I stopped thinking about my previous best friends, Susan, Barbara, and Janine. This day, this day of the dead pony, was day one of working at Mrs. McKay's, a day that changed my life and Kevin's. Of course, she never paid us unless you

consider learning how to ride ponies, milk goats, and treat sick animals pay. They say that what happens to you when you are between 11 and 14 is what forms you for the rest of your life. The universe was watching out for me the day I met Mrs. McKay.

We figured out the quickest route to her house. Leave by the screen porch door and cross the lawn. Duck through the bushes and onto Ruthie's driveway. Head out onto Santa Rosa, go down two houses to Madam Spindler's, and cut through her side yard to the gate that let us into Mrs. McKay's jungle, the northern corner of her five-acre yard. Through the gate we'd go, into the giant bamboo, through the giant fern dell, coming out at the top of her driveway where her three-car garage was, with the red Woody—the wood-paneled station wagon—and her Model Ts. This is where the pens and cages of animals started. This route saved us from having to walk all the way around the block to the beginning of Mrs. McKay's long driveway on Calaveras Street. Kevin and I took it, and in the years to follow, our sister Beth and our brothers John and Mark, two times a day, every day, from the moment we discovered her until well into our teen years.

That summer, Kevin and I became her dedicated workers. We kept going in the fall, which meant getting up before school and hurrying to milk the goats, and hurrying home from school to feed, water, clean and care for her ginormous collection of animals. And, we had a pack of new friends to do it with: Arthur and Judy and Vicki and Jeff, sets of brothers and sisters, like us. Kevin and I thought we knew everything about our neighborhood, yet here was an entirely new world—and just around the corner.

Mrs. McKay lived all alone in her great big house. Her five children were all grown up, and her husband, well, we never knew about him. About Mr. McKay, she just said, "he doesn't like animals." You could tell her house had once been a showplace because there were still remnants of hedged gardens, an exotic orchard, and those stands of bamboo and ferns. Mrs. McKay explained herself by saying, "It all started when my son came home with an Easter bunny, and just little by little, the animals took over."

She loved her animals. Most had been given to her, like the talking raven from an old TV show and the old parade horse, who once wore 250 pounds of silver and pranced in the Rose Parade. The ponies from a pony ride at the zoo.

As for the goats, sheep, chickens, ducks and rabbits, they were not pets. She raised them for her Christian pastor friends, who were involved with something we hadn't heard of called the Heifer Project. Mrs. McKay was like an army general you feared and loved at the same time. The more Kevin and I showed up and proved our reliability to her, the nicer she became. Mrs. McKay started taking us on her outings.

"Kids, fill a box with the littlest chicks and put them in the Woody. Make sure you wash your hands after." She'd look Kevin and me over. "Thank you for wearing clean clothes for our outing." And we'd hop in her station wagon and go off to a charity group where she was the presenter. We would put up her posters of starving children and she'd address the group by cupping a little chick and say to the group, "This chick is a link in a chain of friendship that will one day go around the world. Support the Heifer Project in their mission of ending world hunger." At the end, we helped her collect donations.

Mrs. McKay was always looking for ways to make money. She'd sell the sheep's wool to local weaving and knitting groups. She'd often rent out an upstairs bedroom for extra money and a parade of people came and went. Once she rented to a man with no ear. She had to ask Vito to leave after only a few months because she found vodka bottles in his room. But then she rented to a man with no thumb: He stayed, because everyone fell in love with Mr. Dennis. He was a retired botanist and ex lumber-man (hence the no thumb). Mr. Dennis could grow anything and one of the first things he did was to begin reinvigorating all the old fruit trees. Things came to life I'd never heard of: Green gage plums, Ponderosa lemons, damson plums, persimmons, blood oranges . . . Everything grew for him. Mr. Dennis also had something Mrs. McKay called animal magnetism. We kids loved him but the animals would kind of go crazy trying to get close to him when he passed by their cages and pens, even the guinea pigs. And everyone knows guinea pigs have super tiny brains. To this day Kevin and my sister Beth call themselves Mr. Dennis when they're out in their own gardens, trying to get things to grow.

People came by to buy her goat's milk. There was one customer who Vicki and I couldn't get enough of and we'd find a reason to be in the kitchen when she came over. We'd stare at this large woman in her colorful mumus and bangle bracelets. Her long, thick black hair always looked sweaty. She'd purchase her goat's milk, and then Mrs. McKay would offer her a pint of whey. On the spot, she'd tilt her head back and gulp it all down in one go. Vicki'd whisper into my ear, "Isn't that the grossest thing you ever saw?" One time after she left, Mrs. McKay pulled us aside. "Girls, now listen! You have simply got to be kind to people," she said, sharply, "because you never know. Darla has a health condition, and she's trying her best to cure herself. Her obesity is part of her condition."

As the months wore on, Mrs. McKay became nicer and nicer. We'd sit with the other kids in her kitchen while she fixed us good things to eat. "The most important thing is to always tell the truth," she would say while heating some Monday-Friday soup. She called her soup that because she left it on the stove all week and every day added something new to it. (I know, not refrigerated.) "Because if you can't tell the truth," she continued, "you cannot live by the Golden Rule."

"What's the Golden Rule?" I asked. As she served all of us kids bowls of soup she explained patiently, "It's the one major rule to live by. It means don't do anything to someone that you wouldn't want to have done to yourself. The Golden Rule is very important." Our ears and our minds were open when she spoke to us like this, in a way that they just were not when Mom or Dad or the nuns at school talked.

New in Town

When you've lived in the same place your whole life, your past and your present get intertwined. Today was the day to go find Lisa, an old friend of Michele's and a former high school flame of Jeff's. She'd recently returned to the area. Lisa was part of Jeff's friend group that would pile into his bedroom, turning the gawd awful music up so loud (Ruthie's description for rock 'n roll); come through laughing their heads off at some inside joke and hit the kitchen to eat everything in sight. But Mom was no pushover. "Out!" she'd point to the door. "Everybody go home and eat your own mother's food!" she'd kind of yell—giving them a chance to clear out—before actually really losing it. Funny how I'd inherited so many of Jeff's friends when I moved back to Pasadena in my late 20s, because in high school their wanton rule breaking felt almost terrifying to me. Sure, they'd all go to something so stupid as the prom. But how they hit the thrift stores to garb themselves up in old bride's dresses and top hats. For me, the prom was serious. For me, not pissing off my parents was serious.

Lisa, looking to make a change for herself after years of nine-to-five teaching, now single and with her sons grown, had taken an apartment in a place that seemed like it would provide instant community: a rambling 110-year-old mansion broken into nine apartments. The property still had some gardens and was gated from the busy corner it sat on. The glimpses she caught of the other tenants seemed good to her as she made arrangements just before the pandemic began to rent a ground floor unit with a piece of the garden attached.

Lisa said, "I had envisioned having pizza and beers with my new neighbors in my garden. I'd fixed it with chairs and tables, but everyone was into their own lives, and I couldn't get anyone to actually stop and say hello."

The days of youth, when the object of life seems to be to meet as many people as possible, are long behind many of us. Starting anew is a challenge. Next to Lisa was a single woman, retired from the aerospace industry. Next to her, a man with a PhD in entomology. His back porch was piled with animal cages. Then a 40-something guy who goes out to play tennis a lot. Upstairs and over the garage was an equally eclectic mix of tenants who had busy lives. Added to this were two cats put on the property for mousing (but no kitten project to bring people together).

"There were dribs and drabs of welcome," Lisa said, "but nothing that could move toward relationship. Even the cats were skittish. Then Covid hit. Even though we park our cars next to one another, nobody was doing more than giving a little wave."

Not a happy feeling—knowing that people are so close, just above you, just beside you, but having no relationships with them at all. Then, on NextDoor, she saw a notice about how to host an emergency preparedness meeting. An expert would come out and talk to your group. "I decided to do it," she said. "It was for our own common good, and my likability wasn't at stake. I was just trying to provide something of value to my neighbors.

"I set out chairs and made some cookies, but nothing too much. I didn't want it to seem like I'd fussed or was needy. Almost everybody came! We introduced ourselves. We put our emails and our cell numbers on a sign-up sheet. It was great. From that piece of paper, I created a document for everyone. Now we all keep that list with the emergency supplies we were told to have on hand. Just a few weeks later, when I learned how to get a Covid shot appointment, I sent that info around to all the neighbors, and they were thankful. Now my neighbor above me and I are going to have coffee."

Lisa and I were having coffee together in her spot of garden. Giant schefflera bowered over us, giving the tropical feel that was so loved by the Pasadena mansion owners of 1900. What a lovely thing, to pause in the garden of a friend. Much can come from a coffee or tea break. Wise counsel? Shaking off cares? The launch of an adventure?

I asked Lisa what she thought would make for a fantastic neighborhood. She answered quickly, "Where everyone has a pact with each other to share and barter. Rather than everything being financial transactions, I'd love it if what you needed could be fulfilled by those around you in a friendly sort of way. *Hi, I need a computer guy. Hi, I'm free this afternoon, anybody need a lift? Hi, can anyone fix my fence? Hi, I can hang curtains or prune trees.* To me, that seems wonderful."

There's always the push-pull of being busy. The philosopher Henri Nouwen said we only become neighbors when we are willing to cross the road for one another. That's not so easy when we have our own people to tend to and our own affairs to take care of. But how can we really be neighbors if we don't stop sometimes and see how those nearby are doing? Good going, Lisa.

Bill and I were almost back to the house from a stroll around the block when a white van slowed. Do I know that person? The van pulled over and the window went down—oh my gosh! It was our long-ago neighbor Pam. "It's you!" she called in disbelief. "I'm just driving by our old house! I wanted to see how everything looks after all these years!" We stared in disbelief at one another. "I've wondered about you and Bill so often! You're still here!" Her emotions welled up, she had to take off her glasses. "It's just so nice to see someone from the old days— and right here on the sidewalk! How are your kids?"

"Pam! I know!" I exclaimed. "And your kids?" She wiped her eyes. "Hawaii, New York," she said, throwing her hands out to show how far away they are. "I'm still in Hawaii too, but I'm here because we've moved Mom into Villa Gardens." She put her glasses back on. "I'm so glad Mom's there, it's time, but I just can't bear to leave her."

Oh, the memories flooded. The months and months it took the two of us to read "The Hobbit" aloud to the 6th grade.

She, doing the character voices me, doing the narration. Last-minute knocks on the door to borrow sleeping bags. Me, helping with costumes, she, helping direct all the little plays for our little children at school. . . her Dylan, a Santa. My Grace, a reindeer. . . Her kids were part of that eclipse night, so long ago. Pam, always there across the street during the precious years of raising children and then one day, gone. Poof. Moved away.

Shake Rattle Roll

It's funny business getting prepared for disasters. That oxycodone I kept after oral surgery, it's probably no good anymore—but wait, a friend said, "Oh no, it just gets stronger!" Okay, keep that, because what if I get glass in my feet? But how much good, really, will a bunch of canned goods do if the garage has fallen down around the emergency bin?

We have been warned to be ready for "the big one." Everyone in California knows that's when basically the whole state breaks off into the ocean and everything gets swallowed up. Okay, maybe that won't exactly happen, but there are serious models of all the roads and water and gas lines that will break, serious warnings about fires...

Just looking at a fire extinguisher makes me pray. So I've taken two classes on how to use them, one about 25 years ago, and the other about ten years ago, and each time I left feeling *less* prepared. I heard extinguishers can expire, but I'd have to find the one that's probably in the utility closet or the one that might be buried under the barbecue to see. Yes, the instructors at the classes I took let us squirt the stuff onto the parking lot, but both times I had to think very carefully so as not to shoot the foam right into my own face. Life can be so stressful!

Our neighborhood used to be all about earthquake prep, but there hasn't been an earthquake of consequence for some years now. It's hard staying on the ready for so long. The food expires, the extra cash gets spent, the important papers aren't kept up to date... People's level of preparation pretty much depends on where they live and, more importantly, how vivid an imagination they have. For instance:

Natalia: "We got a generator during the pandemic." "Why?" I wanted to know. "We couldn't tell what was coming and it made us feel safer." "Do you know how to use it?" I asked. Here she chuckled. "No. Ian better be home if we ever need it." Getting a generator during Covid never even occurred to me. We all think so differently.

Brigid: "I always keep jumper cables in the car." "Do you know how to actually use them?" I asked. "Of course. My father really impressed on me the need to know that." When I asked my old friend what else she had on hand in case of disaster, she said, "In my car I always carry flares, a towel, water and flip-flops." "Flip-flops!" I said. "Well," she said, "I might have to get to the beach!"

Jay: "I went out and bought 10 walkie-talkies and distributed them to friends and neighbors. It seemed to me that if our power and internet went out, we'd have a reliable means of communication. It's been awhile, though—I'd better check the batteries."

Paul: "No. No extra food. No extra water." "Really? But don't you feel unprepared?" I asked, remembering he did not grow up in California. He sighed, "I just cannot imagine what could happen that meant I couldn't get water for five days. The way I see it, there are two types of disasters: One that happens to everybody at the same time and one that happens to just you—like, perhaps just your house burns down. I can imagine something happening to just me, so I absolutely have a fire extinguisher." "Do you know where it is?" I asked. "Right here, in the kitchen." Paul got up and walked right to it. This gave me pause. Why are mine so hidden away? Do I even know where they are?

Finally went under the patio counters and pulled out our emergency food supplies, two weeks' worth of canned chili, canned soups and power bars. Everything was past or near its expiration date, but I could not throw it all away. Expiration dates irritate me—I think it's just a way of them getting us to buy things more often. Okay, that spice jar in the cupboard expired in 2015, but a can of tuna six months past? No. Just, no. I spread all the canned goods out on the patio counter and invited our gardeners, Jorge and Javier, to take what they wanted. They took it all. Now, darn it, I have to rebuy the same stuff and put it back under the counter.

"Help! Help!"

Once, Ruthie was completely convinced that someone down the street was being murdered. She hurried from her house and burst into our kitchen, crying out, "Jane! Can't you hear that?"

Mom was at the sink peeling 15 potatoes, like she did so many nights. "No, Mother, I don't hear anything," she said without pausing. I was setting the two tables for dinner. Ruthie, all worked up, started repeating what she'd heard: "Help! Help! Help!" in a sharp, screechy way, all the while trying to get her hearing aids to quit whistling while she spoke.

"Hmm," Mom said, "I have kind of heard that." Mom put the peeled potatoes into the oven. "We've got to call the police!" Ruthie exclaimed.

"Oh Mother, I'm sure it's not that serious."

"How come you're not worried!?" Ruthie cried out and hurried back to her house.

Well, she did call the police because an hour later, the police were ringing our doorbell in the midst of dinner. Everyone jumped up from the tables. Two cops stood in the entryway. "We've investigated a call of a murder in progress," the policeman said to Mom and Dad.

"What?!" they exclaimed.

"A Mrs. Ruth Cassidy called."

"Oh, no, what has Mother done now!" Mom said.

"Based on Mrs. Cassidy's description, we went to the large property on Calaveras Street."

"Mrs. McKay's?" Kevin and I said together.

"Yes, apparently the property owner has several free-roaming peacocks. The owner explained how they send out… well, mating calls at dusk. Some people may think it sounds like a… a mugging. Or a murder." They stifled their laughter. "Good night, folks," they said. Then, openly laughing, they left.

Mom's hands flew to her face, "Oh my god, if Mother doesn't get her hearing aids fixed—" Then the phone rang. "Sally. Answer it," Mom said. Sally went to the phone. "Oh, hello, Mrs. McKay. We are so sorry…"

Well, the next day, when we were working at Mrs. McKay's, she said, "Those policemen last night were very interested in my projects here and asked if I could help them." Later that day, as we were feeding the goats each their sheaf of hay, a police car rumbled slowly up her driveway. We cautiously went to see what was up. Mrs. McKay was always in a dispute with the health department, so policemen made us nervous. Two officers got out of their car and greeted Mrs. McKay. Then one of them opened the back door, reached into the seat, and pulled out a—a pig! A baby pig. "Some hippie thinks he's very funny," the cop said, not amused at all. "We found this in our car the other day and had no idea what to do with it. Glad we found you." He awkwardly handed the little pig off to Mrs. McKay, who took it gladly, and off they went.

"Kids!" Mrs. McKay called in glee. "Look what we've got now!" She hugged the little pig. "Oh, you sweet thing. Let's try putting him in with the goats," she said to us. The goat pen was overcrowded, but that would be changing soon, as one of Mrs. McKay's pastor friends was organizing a trip to an orphanage in Mexico and the goats were going too. We followed her back to the goat pens, and as she clutched the wiggling piglet, she said, "You see, kids? You never know what a new day will bring! You just have to be ready for anything."

Eight Bucks for All of 'Em? Will You Take Five?

The beauty of yard sales is how deep into other people's lives in other parts of town you can go: permission granted to go down someone's driveway, into their back yard—or, if the owner has died, well, then, poke to your heart's content in the house through their winter coats and hobby supplies.

For years, a few friends and I started Saturdays with a cup of coffee for the car and a map of where to go based on ads from the *Pasadena Star-News* or the *Penny Saver.* We knew which parts of town had young families—good for toys and baby needs. We knew the ramshackle parts of town—good for tools and the gems among junk—like, say, a WWII silk map. The best were those with ads like: *Decades of treasures. Everything's gotta go.* That's where to find the treasure you really wished you needed: another set of bone china, champagne glasses still in the wedding gift box, Pendleton blankets for when it snows in LA...

"One of the things that's so fun about yard saling," said Mitch, "is that if you know what sparks joy in your neighbors, what they're looking for, then it's great to come across that thing and call them to say *hurry over before it's gone.* Even better to just show up at their house with it as a big surprise."

Some Saturdays, we'd be in as many as ten different houses in ten different parts of town. Taking a yard-sale home tour puts into relief how it is us—we people with our finite lives—that come and go like the china and the cookware. We occupy a home for a few years or a few decades and then leave, vacating the house for someone else to build their nest in.

Much of LA was built up from the mid 1920s to 1970, long enough for those houses to have sheltered generations of owners. And the heritage houses in the oldest neighborhoods can really tell the tales. Our house has had 130 years of occupants, and sometimes, when I am in a quiet mood, I can feel their presence. How Mr. Larson's back must have hurt as he loaded the basement with barrels of honey in the '70s, satisfying his survivalist needs. How much fun the Halverson kids must have had with the 50 other school-aged children on our block in the '60s. That's when a vacant lot, now the house two doors down, was the group playground for all of them. There is still a neighbor, Bill Loesch, who remembers playing in the oak trees that vacant lot offered. During the Depression, Mr. Pritchard headed out our beveled glass front door every day, walking the two blocks to Lake Avenue, where he'd catch the Red Car and ride it to his downtown LA law office. Or Mr. McPherson, who built our house, how he must have turned the gas lamps up at night as he worked over his drafting table, figuring out the mechanics for the long-gone Mount Lowe Railway, which took tourists up a San Gabriel Mountain peak in the 1890s. Today, a 250-pound piece of his iron gears sits in our garden; it is still here, not disappeared like the so many lives, so many ways of living that went before. The houses hold on, so do the things.

Once, our block organized itself enough to put on a great big communal yard sale. Our lawn was scattered with lamps and upholstered chairs, because we'd redecorated, and things we once thought to be *so* precious were out there with a "make offer" sign. Emily's lawn was filled with kids' toys they no longer used, darling clothes they'd outgrown. Lynnette's yard, bolts of fabric, a coatrack full of odd clothes, bags of zippers. Jama and Joanne's, perfectly great pots, perfectly good propane tanks, woodworking stuff. Other neighbors, not up for a full-on sale of their own, brought their stuff to our lawns to sell off.

We ran back and forth inspecting one another's cast-offs, while fevered buyers drove up, parked, and hurried from one lawn to the next, looking for their version of the Holy Grail. By the end of the day, Lynnette had our matching chairs, which she was excited to reupholster. I had Emily's books for my niece's children. Jama and Joanne had a bolt of Lynnette's tropical fabric for their cabana. It was so successful we decided to do it again in six months...

Mitch and Leslie devised an ingenious way to control the stuff Mitch acquired all year long from yard sales. They'd host a New Year's Day meet-up on their driveway. A sort of friends and neighbors swap meet. Let January begin with a clean sweep. Everyone brought not only their New Year's greetings to one another, but who wants my crock pot? Got a pile of winter clothes here! Bread makers always showed up, and the same ones went round and round. Whatever wasn't swapped right on the spot went right off to charity the next day. It was ingenious.

In 1975, when my parents sold the big house, Mom threw a final *Everything's gotta go* yard sale. Kevin recounted it all to me later because I was living in San Francisco then. Throngs of friends and strangers swarmed the lawn and house. Mom was on a tear to get rid of as much as she could. Without a second glance, out went the huge dining room table that she and her girlfriends had antiqued a silver-blue. Out went the couches she'd reupholstered. Out went table lamps and side tables—even the Chinese lamp she'd meticulously glued back together after a baseball hit it. Paintings, beds, books... all of it. My sibs took a few things but not much, and by the end of the weekend, my parents and brothers and sisters stood around, exhausted. The house was empty. Echo-y empty. There wasn't a single thing left in the big living room except the baby grand piano, which was going to Sally (and then, ten years later, would go to my sister Beth, and then twenty years later, to my niece Tracy).

Kevin sat down and opened the piano and began to play the one song he knew, which he'd tortured us with by playing over and over again—a song he loved from Elvis's Christmas album. Kevin lifted his voice in that stripped bare room as best he could:

I believe for every drop of rain that falls,
a flower grows.
I believe that somewhere in the darkest night,
a candle glows.
I believe for everyone who goes astray, someone will
show the way
I believe, I be—

Mom walked over and closed the keyboard. She sat next to him and began to cry and cry so hard. No one had actually ever seen her do this before. Not when Jim and Jeff were diagnosed with type 1 diabetes. Not when baby Michael, three days old, died. Not even when John died in the accident . . . She kept it from us. Kevin, Sally, Jeff, Dan, Beth, Mark, Jim—just stood there. "It's just like when I was nine—when they took everything—."

"What are you talking about, Mom?" everyone cried.

"On Riverside Drive in New York. Our apartment with the ten-foot ceilings. Mother and I stood there and watched them take everything away. Daddy went to jail. The stock market had crashed. The movers came. Rolled up the Persian carpets, took away the big Ming vases, took everything and when they left our apartment it was as empty as this. All we had was money for the bus—to California and live with Aunt May. I didn't see Dad for six years." Kevin told me everyone stood there wide-eyed as she cried her eyes out. Mom could not wait to unburden herself from that house, but she just didn't realize what it really meant, how much it would hurt.

I do not want to own a lot of precious things that I have to be responsible for. I began pulling things out of drawers and decided to deliver a gift to the little girl turning ten at the end of the block. They were tiny, hand-blown glass vases from Venice. Exquisite. The size of your thumb, perfect for a child to daydream over. I'd had them tucked away long enough. Maybe she has so much stuff that they'll be meaningless, but maybe not. When I was ten, Mrs. Hertel gave me a pair of pierced earrings. They were real gold and lacquer from her travels to China. Holding them in my small hand was like holding a passport to where she'd been. Of course they were too grown-up for me, but she must have had them tucked away long enough. I have never forgotten her gift.

For Everything There Is a Season

Donna. I hadn't seen Donna in years, but she was only a few blocks away. Like me, her children were grown, and she was on to other things. But I knew she stayed in connection with her immediate neighbors and in fact most of those on her block have breakfast together once a month, in one another's houses, like for more than 20 years now.

It was a quiet pandemic morning the day we met up on her sidewalk to take a stroll. Donna began pointing out her neighbors. "Bev—across the street— has lived here the longest, forty years," she said. "David lives two doors down. We're constantly saying to each other, *You've got to make things fun.* And you know what? You do. It only takes one or two extroverts to get things going," Donna said. "Think about it, in a group of ten one's an extrovert and the other nine are grateful."

"That's a good one," I laughed in reply. Donna continued energetically, "My mother-in-law—I learned from her—consistently invited the neighbors to dinner. Does anyone do *that* anymore?" "But Donna, everyone is so busy today," I said. Donna wouldn't buy it. "Today, I think people forget that neighbors are important. Mary Lea, everyone has the choice of watching another TV show or making a chicken dinner and inviting someone in. Which thing in the long run makes for higher satisfaction?"

"Still," I said. "It can be a lot."

"I know, but my mother-in-law totally knew how to fix that," Donna announced. "She had six recipes. That was it. Any one of them she could make for four, she could make for 40, and she'd rotate them depending on who she was having over." Donna counted the recipes out on her fingers. "Apricot chicken. Pork tenderloin—either with orange marinade, cranberry marinade, an almond crust, or a sesame seed crust. Beef ribs. Baked chicken. Beef stroganoff. Sausage zucchini soup. Then, lots of salad, lots of bread, lots of wine. Done." How can someone not love Donna?

For several months I thought about Donna's comment about how you need a few extroverts and you need to keep it fun if you want to bring people together. Well, she could have been talking about Suzanne. I used to call Suzanne the Martha Stewart of our neighborhood, much the way my old neighbor, Pam, used to call me the Yellow Pages, because she looked to me on who to call for problems: plumber? handyman? rat trouble?

Suzanne and I took a walk the other day. Like so many friends, I don't see her as much as I'd like. She came up my way from a few blocks away. Walking is no longer easy for her, but her doctor said *Do It!* As we passed a taupe and grey two-story Craftsman, she said, "What do you hear of Kellye?" That Craftsman had been Kellye's house. The first house to ever get fixed up in this neighborhood. But Kellye'd moved to another part of town about ten years ago.

"Oh, Suzanne. Didn't you hear? Kellye died."

"What?" she cried. "Nobody told me!"

There was a time when this type of news would have spread instantly. I shook my head, "I know. Nobody told me either. I heard about it while watching the Academy Awards, that part at the end, the *In Memoriam* part." Kellye had been such a big presence to so many of us, often gardening out front, talking to everyone who passed by. She loved to paint a watercolor of someone's house and give it to them as a gift. She was an artist and a teacher, became a movie extra and then an actual actress on the TV show M*A*S*H. Kellye became Nurse Kellye.

Shaking her head Suzanne said, "She mentored me when I went back to school for my teaching credential. So generous."

Yes, there was a time when this type of news would be shared and responded to within minutes, back when Suzanne and I were home with small children...

Back in the early '90s, when I was out on the sidewalk pushing a stroller with my toddler and new baby, a woman called out to me from across the street. "Hey, you should join us for playgroup." She too was pushing a stroller. "We meet Tuesday mornings. Tomorrow, it's at Suzanne's." She

crossed the street, introduced herself as Peggy and her tiny son as Ryan, and quickly wrote out an address. "9 a.m. It's a lot of at-home moms living within walking distance." Really? There were other women at home all day with small children? I had felt quite completely alone in this quiet neighborhood with my two little girls.

The next day, my bulging stroller and I showed up at a house close by. I could hear a gathering going on out back, and since the door was ajar, I simply pushed on through and out to the deck.

As a new mom, suddenly at home after years of career work, I was feeling a stark loss of identity and as if I no longer had friends. So, when I stepped out onto Suzanne's deck, filled with nice-looking, smart women, all engaged in mothering small children and enjoying coffee and conversation, I felt like I was being thrown a life jacket.

Suzanne, with a baby at her breast, called out a hearty *hello there!* A dozen other moms did the same. This was a playgroup started by one woman who knew she needed friends and knew it was up to her to find them. What she did was, whenever she saw another woman pushing a stroller through the neighborhood, she'd invite them to join her. The only criterion was you had to walk to playgroup. She didn't want to get to know women and children from all over the place, she just wanted to know those who lived nearby. Lucky me, I had just walked into a friend group that would sustain me for the next two decades.

I complimented Suzanne on her coffee. I complimented her on all the sweet rolls. I complimented her on her spacious deck. On her many fruit trees. On her matching tablecloths on the various tables. To each compliment she said, as if it were just nothing – "Oh, thanks. I made it." Or "thanks, I planted them," or "thanks, I sewed them," or "thanks, I built it." Who was this person? How could we become friends? This new group made me realize how much I had to learn.

But really what Suzanne showed all of us was how to simply open our doors to others. Have people inside without a lot of fussing. There was always a spot at her kitchen table, and the tea kettle was always ready to be fired up. Once, when she was out front on Thanksgiving morning, a couple she didn't recognize strolled by. She called out "Happy Thanksgiving! Where do you guys live?" They said they'd just moved here. Suzanne couldn't help herself and said, "Want to come to our house for Thanksgiving?" She didn't think they'd actually say yes, but they did!

I think of all the activities that sprang from that playgroup: The 4th of July street party, the revitalization of the neighborhood Halloween, the Thursday-night porch parties, where close-in neighbors dropped by; even the neighborhood association's home tour, which grew to attract hundreds. All these activities began over one or two of us having a conversation.

Our kids from that playgroup played together. There was a difference between the friends from school and the friends from the neighborhood. At school, it really was only the kids from your grade, and then only if the chemistry worked. In the neighborhood, it was boys and girls, younger and older, selected by how close you lived to one another, not by how alike you were. I've always thought that children get a stronger sense of place in the world if they simply walk to a friend's house rather than go to a playdate that we adults arranged. Sometimes those neighborhood friendships stretched far into adulthood.

Our three girls were tiny when Sara's mom, Rita, proposed a fancy Christmas "teddy bear tea" to about six of us moms. We poured apple juice into toy teacups, and the girls each brought a favorite doll or teddy bear. We mothers could barely stand how cute it was. Over time, they graduated to actual English tea, and the dolls and stuffed toys became more decoration than companion. Over more time, the little girls grew to be young women, away at college, and then working, but sure to make it home for the Christmas tea. Teddy bears and dolls were no longer on the scene; they held a cup of tea in one hand and a glass of champagne in the other. We, the now-older moms, could barely stand how gorgeous, mature, accomplished these onetime playmates now were. A lawyer, a chef, a journalist, a teacher, a gardener, an artist. . . To witness the growth of people you have known since they were tiny is as deeply satisfying a sight as life can offer. A simple, profound pleasure not possible without the benefit of being in one place long enough to witness it, or by stirring yourself to stay in connection with those who have moved or changed.

When the "new" family next door arrived, their baby was in diapers, not able to get up the front steps. In a twinkling he was the boy on the skateboard. A nano-moment later, the taillights of his car passed by. Nobody young believes it, but everybody old knows it: Life unfolds so very quickly and then goes.

Suzanne and I finished our walk 'n talk after zigzagging through the neighborhood, ending back at her house. "My doctor's going to be glad—almost 5,000 steps," she said heartily, checking her Fitbit. We gave each other a warm air-hug and I headed on.

While on my walk, I spied a beautiful geranium blooming in Mike and Ann's yard; not really their yard, more their parkway. It is a unique maroon color and I wanted some for my yard. Would it be okay to just take a little cutting—no harm, no foul? After all, it was kind of hanging over the sidewalk. And it is just a geranium cutting. But what if it were my geranium, and I saw a neighbor helping herself? Long ago, I had learned the basics of The Golden Rule . . . so I went and knocked on Ann's door and asked permission.

Escaped Ponies

We all knew the pony pen was no Fort Knox—part chain link, part old doors, part vertical fencing. The gaps were crisscrossed with wire, the falling down parts propped up with limbs from the eucalyptus that had broken off. Mrs. McKay had asked us to fix up the fencing several times, but it just seemed hard to do and not fun, and also, the wood pile from which to draw supplies was full of black widows. Her five ponies resided in her former rose garden, now a large dusty arena. Most of the time, the ponies seemed too sleepy and a little too stupid to try anything new. The problem that spring, though, was lots of tall green grass growing on the other side of the fence, in a vacant part of Mrs. McKay's yard that faced the street. A tidy row of post-1945 houses was across the street, mostly occupied by people we kids didn't know.

The day it happened, Ginger was the first to leap straight over to get the grass—we watched her, like some kind of giant wind-up toy, jump from a placid standstill and just sail over. And as soon as she did that, the light bulb went on with the other ponies. Smoky, Wampum, Patches, and Skyrocket followed right behind her, but they didn't stop to eat the grass. No! They careened straight down the yard and on into the street. Oh no!

Poor Patches was so old that she foundered and fell down. But she got back up. If the ponies could've high-fived each other they would have, so spirited was their charge into the street. Patches headed down the nearest driveway, while Wampum crashed through a flimsy picket fence. We ran after them with a backwards yell to Arthur: "Tell Mrs. McKay! Get the halters! Get ropes!"

Soon Mrs. McKay was on the street too. Then the neighbors were out, waving their arms. "Oh, why didn't we fix the fence when she told us to?" I called to Vicki and Kevin as we ran after them.

"Who knew they could jump like that?" Vicki called back.

We split up. I went down someone's driveway after Patches, who was standing like a confused statue in the middle of a man's lawn. "What the heck?" the man said, stepping out onto his back porch. "Sorry. So sorry," I said slipping the halter around her ears.

"You kids got to be more careful!" he called. *Why do adults always state the obvious*, I thought, nodding apologetically as I tugged Patches away.

I could see Kevin a few doors down with a rope around Ginger's neck, nodding contritely to a flustered lady. Where was Wampum? And Skyrocket? And Smoky? We all stood for a minute in the middle of the street. Where'd they go? "Kids, we've got to get back and wait for the phone to ring," Mrs. McKay said. "And start on the fence. Now listen," she said, as two ponies and four kids anxiously followed her up the driveway, "if you'd fixed the fence on Saturday we wouldn't be in this mess today. See how you've made so much extra work for yourselves by not taking care of things right away?"

The phone was already ringing when we got to the kitchen. "Mary Lea, go get Smoky out of Madame Spindler's garden." I ran through the jungle and through the gate dividing their properties. Smoky was a really small pony. He could only be ridden by a kid who was less than 100 pounds. There he was, trapped in her rose bushes. Madame Spindler was coming out. Oh, now I was trapped! "Come inside and have a cookie," she said in her screechy German accent. "Tie him to the mailbox. Come in." Mrs. McKay had told us to be nice to her and it would be impolite to say no, so I followed her into the dim and cold kitchen. She'd lived all alone for years but taught opera singing to people who came over. She handed me a crumbly cookie from an almost-empty jar. "Let me show you the pictures of my daughter, the singer," she began. *Oh no, here we go. . .* And now I'm looking at Elisa, who sings in Vienna and Milan and New York. . .

What I was really looking at was Madame Spindler's red, scaly legs coming up from her house slippers. And what was under her loose-fitting dress? Could it be a beach ball? Her fuzzy grey hair up in a knot, like always. Why did her eyes water and bug out like that? I took in the big round diamonds that dangled from her long ears. It must be completely horrible to be that old, and I knew in my twelve-year-old heart that I'd never let getting-old happen to me.

"Thank you, Madame. I better get back. Two ponies are still missing."

"You chill-den are so sweet. Stop in again soon. Bye-bye." She waved at me until I was through the gate.

By the time I returned with Smoky, Mrs. McKay already had the red Woody fired up. "Skyrocket made it all the way up to Altadena Drive. You and Vicki hop in." So while Kevin, Arthur, and Judy worked on the fence, we rode up to Mrs. Nelson's, a sort-of friend of Mrs. McKay's. She was a rich old lady with hedged gardens. Back in the Depression, Mrs. McKay had been rich too because Mr. McKay had been in nickel plating. She had a nickel-plated tea set to prove it. But by the 1960s, when we knew her, that was all gone and the animals were her life. Her five grown-up children, like Madame Spindler's daughter, visited rarely.

Mrs. McKay didn't stop in. "Tell her hello," she said, letting me and Vicki out. We went to the door carrying a rope and a halter. "Come in kids," Mrs. Nelson said in a chilly voice. She wore a pink pants suit and a lot of gold bracelets. "He's back by the pool."

Skyrocket was so alert and excitable that we had to approach him very carefully so he wouldn't do something stupid, like dash into the pool. "Easy. Easy, boy," I said, feeling proud of myself that I'd gotten so good at this over the past year. "Vicki, other side." We had our hands out, our voices soft. Skyrocket looked to me, looked to Vicki, and bolted! Straight into the side of Mrs. Nelson's car!

Her shiny, fancy car. But he was cornered, and we quickly got him into a halter. Vicki and I felt so accomplished as we walked this pretty black pony the almost mile home. Drivers smiled and waved to us as they slowed to admire Skyrocket and we smiled and waved back.

"Now, kids," Mrs. McKay said, once it was all over and we were sitting around the red booth in her kitchen. What a world that kitchen was, with its red Formica counters and two sinks, the freezer locker by the back door and next to it a real soda fountain from a real soda shop. It worked when her children were little but now it was piled high with old National Geographics. She'd handed out big bowls of her soup. The parrot cage and the aquarium had a place in the kitchen too, along with tall stacks of newspapers and piles of coupons she clipped. Mrs. McKay often stood at her kitchen counter clipping articles about world peace and world starvation, her two main interests. She'd put the best pictures of starving children into her binder. Mrs. McKay had been a nurse and knew all the different names for starvation. Kwashiorkor. Marasmus. Anemia. She'd make us say them so we pronounced them correctly. She sat with us on a red folding kitchen stool. "Let's think about today," she said. "What happened?" Nobody answered right away because her soup was so delicious.

"We put off a small job so it became a big job," Kevin said.

"Good," Mrs. McKay said. "So, how's the fence?"

"We finished," Judy said.

“Are all the ponies fed? Do they seem alright?” she asked. We all nodded yes. Mrs. McKay enjoyed some of her own soup and then said something that went straight into all of our hearts. “You are very good kids.”

Everyone Has a Hand in Halloween

Back in the early '60s, Mom got so upset when she heard our town's historic theater had gone bankrupt. But she wasted no time in hopping into her rumbly Cadillac and getting to the closing-down sale early. The theater was selling off everything and oh, the treasures she came home with! An actual real fake pirate's chest, which she'd filled with handfuls of costume jewelry from the 1920s, and real flapper dresses of chiffon, and a real suede toreador's outfit. Plus, turquoise cowboy boots, velvet capes, a top hat, and more!

My parents never had an extra dime. No matter how hard Dad worked, there was always a new baby and another bill that barely got paid. Mom did all kinds of things to bring in extra money: write publicity pieces for little businesses, sell Christmas cards to wealthy ladies, sell ads for the local newspaper. Sometimes she'd get dressed up and MC a fashion show for Catholic Charities and get a new dress out of the deal. Mom could economize on anything, but she also knew when money just had to be spent. After all, she was the daughter of Ruthie, with just enough of Ruthie's movie star ways.

“Help me with this, kids,” Mom said as she threw open the back doors of her purple Caddie with the broken top. “Let’s carry it right up to the attic.”

“What’s in it! What’s in it?” we all wanted to know. A bunch of us helped carry the pirate’s chest up to the third-floor attic.

“Now,” she said, pausing so we’d lean in closer. “Let’s open it.” She dramatically fiddled with the lock and then allowed us to help open it up. The profusion of costumes was dazzling. “It’s all for you,” she exclaimed. “Halloween’s coming!”

We could barely wait until the night itself. As soon as it got dark, off with our pillowcases we went, not coming back until every neighbor’s house went dark. For three hours we did our best to hit every house up and down Santa Rosa, and on every side street, too. We liked the close together houses better because you could get candy quicker than from the old houses with long driveways. Plus, old people lived in the old houses. Madame Spindler gave out one old cookie from her stale cookie jar. The reclusive widow across from Susan didn’t even know it was Halloween. A flapper, a cowboy and a toreador had to explain it to her. Not wanting to disappoint, she got her pocketbook and pulled out a pack of cigarettes. She dropped one cigarette into each of our pillowcases.

❀

On one of our morning walks I asked Janet, who lives three blocks away, to tell me again how the pumpkins started. Obligingly, she recounted, "Must have been about 30 years ago when Sherry and family moved in behind Ben and me. They talked gardening through the chain link fence. Finally, Sherry cut away the vines and put a gate in and a real friendship began over gardening." I nodded as we strolled. "Ben was good with vegetables, herbs and fruit trees," she continued, "but what Sherry brought to the neighborhood were the big pumpkins." I nodded with pleasure. I knew this story well. I loved those gargantuan pumpkins. Pumpkins big enough for Cinderella to ride in if only they'd had wheels. For the next ten years, Sherry and Ben grew these Halloween behemoths and shared them around.

Our kids loved watching them grow in Ben's yard and would get their wagon and head to his house when a choice monster had been selected. Tipping the wagon on its side, Ben would lift it in, then it was up to them to pull it two blocks uphill to home. There, Bill and I lifted it onto our front steps and—presto—Halloween was on!

I love this spontaneous, out-of-bounds holiday almost more than Christmas. But in the '90s, when the children were very little, it scared me to hear other mothers say things like, "I'll *never* let my children trick or treat! Did you hear about the abduction? Did you hear about the poison? Omg, the candy!— *Their teeth*!" True, some stories of horrible things had happened on this night but, no trick-or-treating? Was fear allowing this beloved holiday to fade away?

Something had to be done. Purely to offer my own children the magic I'd always felt for Halloween, I put a plan before the neighborhood mother's group. "What if everyone meets on our front lawn at five o'clock? Let's do hotdogs and cider. Make sure the kids eat a little something solid and then everyone trick-or-treat together?"

The first year our lawn party attracted about 5 kids and their parents, but word spread. It didn't matter to me who came, invite your friends, your friend's friends—just come and let's make it fun! With this type of invitation, everyone wanted to help. Three days in advance of the holiday, neighbors began dropping off bags of supplies: apple juice, packs of hotdogs, buns, relish, a gallon or two of milk. So, the next year about 25 kids and their parents showed up. Early afternoon of Halloween, neighbors who were free helped drag out the folding tables, helped make the hotdogs and mix up the cider. I added chili to the menu because adults needed more than just hotdogs...

Oh how this plan worked. Right at five o'clock cars began pulling up. Out hopped little goblins and princesses as if they were hopping out of little forest homes. From the gathering dusk came little Power Rangers and pirates, hurrying down the sidewalk or from out nearby doorways. Parents appeared, carrying trays of macaroni and cornbread. From around the corner came an entire *Addams Family.* Here comes a child in a refrigerator packing box, painted like a refrigerator with food taped inside, here comes Dorothy in spray-painted ruby slippers. By year four, the entire front lawn filled up with merry-scaries. But it all seemed quite controllable because the party lasted just an hour. At the stroke of six everyone was off. These little aliens and Darth Vaders had work to do!

Our front porch filled up too, with friends who situated themselves around a crockpot of potent mulled wine. They'd come to our house because wherever it was they lived, no trick-or-treaters came. Convivially, they'd watch the parade of costumed children march up and down our front steps with their bags out. And as the level of hot mulled wine went down in the crockpot, enthusiasm for the really good costumes went up, the best garnering applause: the two boys in a cardboard boat who "rowed" from house to house. The boy as an astronaut in an outfit made from cereal boxes sprayed silver. *Little House On the Prairie* girls pulling a real covered wagon. Some costumes seemed ever popular, dead cheerleaders, Chuckie masks, and good ol' witches in pointy hats.

But after that fourth year, I did get a little scared. How many Halloween celebrators did we actually have? What if it kept growing like this? Hotdogs and chili are not loaves and fishes and so the strategy became "the first 100 eat." That's how I counted heads, by making 100 hotdogs and 10 pounds of chili, the first 100 who showed up, ate. But strangely just when the last hotdog got plucked from the pot of hot water, a parent seemed to show up with a pizza or another tray of hotdogs "just in case."

Inevitably, as the years passed, our children grew beyond trick-or-treating and the lawn party baton passed to the Fergusons on the corner. There, this tradition carried on until their children too, grew beyond... but by then neighbors all around had embraced the spirit. Since I was always so busy answering the door, I'd never taken a Halloween stroll through my own neighborhood until a few years ago. It amazed me how lively all the decorated houses were, the witty headstones in lawns, card tables set at the ends of driveways with costumed adults laughing and talking, giving out candy or a sly cup of wine for adults. Fog machines? Live music from someone's porch? Welcome mats that scream when you step on them? Yes, all of it—everywhere. And to think that in the early '90s, this holiday was in danger of fading into the past.

No trick or treating this year because of Covid. Oh, the poor kids on our block! At first my feeling was just let the holiday go this year, everything feels pretty quiet, people probably don't want to bother. But then I did finally reach out, last minute, to the parents of those kids—and several other neighbors; how wrong I was— everyone was game to make it nice for the kids. Together we planned a scavenger hunt for them. The enthusiasm to make Halloween fun in this weird year felt wonderful. Adults up and down the block hid treats in their front yards, around the cars in driveways and up in trees.

Home for the Holidays

The second year of the pandemic is winding down, and here it is—another day, another walk, this time around the block to say hi to Ginger and Bill. Yes, I was thinking of Halloween—and the 4th of July, and Easter, and Christmas—all the holidays we mark our year with and decorate for. Despite his issues with diabetes, including a kidney transplant, nothing stops Bill and Ginger's efforts to create big, zany holiday lawn displays. This is living out front in a big way, and they've done it especially big during these last two years of isolation.

It'd been ages since I'd seen them, ages since the kids grew up, but it was easy to call them. And now here we were, sitting on their front wall in the late afternoon. I wanted to know more about their ever-growing themed displays. After all, it takes them a full year to develop and stage them. "One year Bill picks the theme, the next year I pick," Ginger explained. "So one year it's *Hocus Pocus*, the next year it's *Tombstone*, and so on."

"How did this get started?" I asked.

"Our house was already known as the haunted house when we bought it," Ginger said, chuckling. "And we thought—well, let's have fun with that."

"Wait, haunted? Remind me," I said.

"Well, a previous owner died right here." She pointed to the front porch.

Ginger and Bill's house, from about 1910, is poured concrete with a heavy, overhanging balcony. The lawn is big enough to handle an eighty-foot deodar tree, and in the back, there still exists an honest-to-goodness carriage house with a forge. "The earliest owners built their own cars in the garage and used the forge to hand-make the parts," Bill explained. "All the first cars in LA were made in people's back yards."

"After we moved in," Ginger continued, "Mrs. Walker, who lived kitty corner from us—she's passed away now—came over to tell us about the horrible death. The man was leaning over the balcony railing. We don't know how but for whatever reason, he fell over and landed on his head right here on the front steps." Bill and Ginger paused, sort of shivered, but she continued on cheerfully, "So we've made the most of the haunted thing." Very few homeowners would want to "make the most of the haunted thing," but Bill and Ginger are exceptional.

Their Halloween vignettes started simply with flying ghosts on a pulley system going up and down through the deodar tree with lights and music. That was wonderful enough but they got increasingly ambitious, creating action scenes like a dune buggy crash with skeletons and a real dune buggy. Or a skeleton tractor driver off-loading coffins, using a real, old-fashioned tractor. Or zombies—full-sized zombies—escaping their graves, which Bill dug into his lawn. There was the prom night car wreck (the dune buggy was back; empty booze bottles, skeletons, bloody tuxes and torn dresses). "Hocus Pocus," from the classic Halloween film, so fun; the three witches riding a vacuum, a broom and a mop, way up in the deodar. The vignettes have spread to their neighbors' lawn as well. After all, if you're going to fully re-create the Shootout at the OK Corral, you need to spread out.

"The whole scene was with *skeletons*," Bill says with glee. "Our basement's full of props, costumes and clothes I hunt for all year," adds Ginger. "For the OK Corral scene, I aged the clothes with hot black tea and antiqued all the props for the saloon." They'd spent the previous summer building a jail, a saloon, an undertaker's office, and a Wells Fargo false front. (Mostly they get their building supplies from other people's old fences.) Every year, when Halloween is done, in a twinkling they turn whatever tableau they've created into a Christmas scene. The year of the OK Corral, the saloon became Mrs. Claus's kitchen, and the Wells Fargo front became the elves' workshop. "We had to switch to mannequins though because, duh, skeletons aren't Christmassy," Ginger said, and they both laughed at the notion.

From October to New Year's, groups of people stroll by or drive into the neighborhood to admire first the car crashes or zombies, then life at the North Pole. "We have a lot of fun doing this," they said almost together. "It gives people pleasure."

As we sat out in front, on the low wall, many a friendly dog walker passed by. I asked them about the community dog-poop trash can they'd installed on the telephone pole. "I got so tired of people complaining on NextDoor about how *Somebody put their dog poop baggie in my trashcan!* that I just decided to do something about it," Ginger said. "What's the big deal if someone drops a baggie into your trash bin? *People*— it gets picked up every Wednesday!

"The funny thing," she added, "is now so many more dog walkers walk here because of the convenience so now it overflows! But we deal with it. I like to see all the types of dogs that come by."

I asked what they thought made a good neighborhood. "Pride. Pride in your surroundings," Bill said without hesitation. Ginger added, "But also, what are you willing to give up? People can be so angry—those who don't like dogs. Don't like loud music. Don't like others' barbecue smoke! For a neighborhood to work in a wonderful way, you have to be willing to give some things up. You have to really think before complaining. Yes, it is your property, but does it have to be your kingdom? If you cannot give up complaining, then no neighborhood will ever be good enough."

Bill agreed, with a quick paraphrase from Proverbs: "And if you have trouble with your neighbor, go and speak to him directly."

"Exactly," Ginger agreed. "For instance, our neighbor has two big, loud parties a year. Only two. And somebody always calls the cops. Come on! It's two times a year, what is the problem?"

What is the problem? The problem is . . . us. The challenge of living in harmony. The challenge of not sweating the small stuff. The challenge when one person sees red and the other person sees blue—but we're looking at the same thing! That's why I love these two neighbors who spend much of the year concocting silly, amazing holiday displays. Their work says, *Come on people—let's enjoy ourselves. Let's lighten up.*

The sun was hitting low in the camphor trees. I was saying my goodbyes when a little boy slowly approached to ask if Ginger and Bill had found a giraffe on their grass. His dad stood nearby. The little boy said he'd lost it at Christmas. Bill and Ginger put on sober faces to show him they took his loss seriously. They glanced around their lawn, but Ginger had to say, "No, we're sorry, we didn't find your giraffe," and his dad led him off. Another couple, jogging by, paused to ask how Bill was feeling. He smiled and nodded, "Kidney's doing fine."

I headed for home calling over my shoulder, "Take care, you guys. Thanks for the visit . . ."

5:30 am. Laced my tennis shoes and headed out onto the sidewalk. Sun's not yet up but the air is clean and ready. The trees are still in black silhouette but the pearls and corals of dawn are appearing. I stroll right down the middle of the street and clasp my hands behind me.

The pandemic, the scared craziness of the early pandemic is gone and we're figuring out how to live with it. Doctors do say we'll be dealing with it for a long time though. But however it plays out, here we all are, once again running around busy as ever. Gone seems to be the time to watch the birds, do something extra for a neighbor... call an old friend just because...

And it makes me wonder. Do the small interactions between us and between neighbors add up? The greetings, the good intentions, the willingness to help, can such a small thing as saying hello be of consequence? Nice for a moment, sure, but the ripple is so minuscule that soon the pool looks as still as ever. It's much like the sidewalks. Though I have walked them a thousand times there is no trace of a footprint...

Makes me wonder as I stroll quietly, picking my way past houses and trees, lawns and walls, finding my way through my own society that feels increasingly unreliable. So many things to separate us besides a mysterious virus. We each have a list of what challenges us, of what we can't understand in another. But as road markers on how to thrive, I rely on the little 'how 'ya doings?' The offerings of 'sure, I'll get your mail.' The invitation to 'let's grab a coffee' that each day might bring. Often these tiny exchanges happen on the common ground of our neighborhoods. I feel affirmed in these little meetups and that yes, in fact, we are all rowing the same big boat together.

Not long ago, I took a flight. It had been two years since boarding a plane and I stared out the window as we flew low across Los Angeles before gaining altitude to head across the country. Hundreds of thousands of housetops were below me. Plenty of tiny blue pools. Plenty of tiny green trees that line the countless streets. Within this maze, millions of people, like you and like me, are living their lives. Do most of them think what I'm thinking, I wondered? That we need each other and it's to our peril if we can't act like it?

Seems to me that one big job for us all, above the regular daily responsibilities of life, is to spread goodwill—love actually, in all its varied forms— to whoever we might come in contact with. What if everybody, absolutely everybody, were thinking this— and tried every single day to spread goodwill? What if a smile really could change the course of history? We know it can change the course of a day— so what if we found ourselves doing this big job all together en masse, what kind of world would it be? Hard to imagine, but I think it'd be like heaven.

The End

Acknowledgments

Creative accomplishments don't happen single handedly. No, no, there are legions of helpers—some offering simple words of encouragement and others, giving long hours of themselves to the project. One such person would be Janet Nippell, who put her trained editing and organizing skills to this difficult to wrangle project. *Across the Street Around the Corner* seems like a smooth, even simple endeavor now but trust me, it emerged from quite an array of moving parts. Along with Janet, there is also Colleen Dunn Bates, a beacon of knowledge and generosity who, as my former publisher, offered without hesitation her final editing skills and opened channels to a new publishing home. These two, wow, without these two I'd just be home weeding roses.

This book is filled with dozens of neighbors and friends who are people to be admired; each taking baby steps in making life better for others. Whether they actually see it that way or not, they are. Each spent precious time with me in conversations which I could then employ in creating a book that hopefully will bring happiness to readers.

I would like to thank the Clyde Custom Publishing editorial and design team, including Rachel Bell, Patrick McDonald,

Deja Nick, Maria Antonio, Sean Paul Lavine, Chloe Lineberg, Emma Malinoski, Tyler Caldwell, Emily Raychaudhuri, Taylor Belgrade, and Megan Jacobs.

And lastly to Bill and our well-grown daughters—Glennie, Grace and Rose. May they create community in whatever neighborhoods they find themselves in. Thank you, reader, for spending time with me in *Across the Street Around the Corner.* May it bring pleasure and joy.